D1260747

Pennsylvania Fireside Tales Volume IV

(Origins & Foundations of Old-time Pennsylvania Mountain Legends & Folktales)

By Jeffrey R. Frazier

Author of:
Pennsylvania Fireside Tales
The Black Ghost of Scotia & More Pennsylvania Fireside Tales
Pennsylvania Fireside Tales Volume III

Still the pine woods scent the noon, still the catbird sings his tune;
Still autumn sets the maple forest blazing,
Still the grapevine through the dusk flings her soul-compelling musk;
Still the fireflies in the corn make night amazing!

They are there, there, there with Earth immortal
(Citizens, I give you friendly warning).
The things that truly last when man and times have passed
They are all in Pennsylvania this morning.

Rudyard Kipling

Pennsylvania Fireside Tales Volume IV

By Jeffrey R. Frazier

Egg Hill Publications
113 Cottontail Lane
Centre Hall, Pa. 16828

Second Printing
Printed in the United States of America
Jostens Commercial Publications
401 Science Park Road
State College, Pa. 16803

All photos by the author, unless otherwise noted.

ISBN 0-09652351-5-7

Cover:
Henry and Mrs. Myrtle Eyer
(Pine Mountain, Clinton County, about 1935)
Mrs. Eyer is still remembered today for the excellent baked goods she always had on hand to offer to visitors who stopped by the Eyer farm when passing over the mountain on the Pine-Loganton Road.
Mr. Eyer's story of an unusual method of capturing a bear is recalled in the last chapter of this volume.
(Photo courtesy of the Annie H. Ross Library, Lock Haven)

Previous page:
Pioneer Pennsylvania hunter taking aim at a panther
- see "big Cats of the Big Woods" (chapter VIII)
(Drawing by James Frazier).

To Clarence Musser, Jared Ripka, Abraham Lincoln Maurer, Clayton Auman, J. Ernest Wagner, Randall Steiger, L. W. Bumbaugh, Cliff Vonada, Nellie Jack, and many other old-time mountain folks like them who shared their stories with me over the years.

Table of Contents

List of Photographs / Illustrations

INTRODUCTION TO VOLUME IV

"Why does he want to do that?", someone once asked my wife, after she told them I was collecting and writing about the folktales and legends of Pennsylvania. At first it seemed like an odd query, but as I thought about it I realized it's a question that deserves an answer, especially for anyone who had not grown up in the Pennsylvania hills of fifty-five or more years ago.

Times have changed so much and so fast since that period that it's somewhat unpleasant to look at the way things are now and compare them to even what it was like when I was a teen. Back then the landscape seemed to me to be composed only of rolling fields, peaceful farms, and small country hamlets surrounded by towering mountains and dense woodlands. Those who lived in this high country of windy knolls and serene mountains were mainly the descendants of the state's original settlers, and when, in 1970, I started to talk to them about local legends and folktales, there were still many older people alive who were not that many decades removed from the time when their ancestors came here and claimed the mountains as their own.

Older people like that continue, in most cases, to be my best sources of material, and although I still enjoy interviewing younger people today I find that as the years roll by it is that oldest generation I first interviewed, the great-grandparents and great-great-grandparents of those alive today, that I've liked the best. These older folks always seemed more appreciative of our beautiful Pennsylvania hills and more contented with a simpler style of living than the hard-driven people of today. Theirs, however, is a time that has vanished, and I've always felt sad that I couldn't have experienced their way of life and that time of life more personally. It's their stories that help me to do that, even if just in a small way, and it's nice to be able to pick up my books and visit with those old folks whenever I feel the need to travel back to their time and place. However my desire to preserve the old tales and legends is not based solely on a need to satisfy my own pangs of nostalgia.

Another objective I've always had in mind in writing my volumes is to preserve the old stories and local color to show younger generations what life was once like in these hills when times were far different than they are today. Sixty-five years ago my father was using a team of horses to plow his father's fields, and now, as the number of small farmers continues to diminish at an alarming rate, I look back and remember how green my valley once was. It is my hope that, in some small way, my books will inspire future generations to appreciate our state's natural heritage and to fight for its preservation, a trend which perhaps will accelerate as non-natives continue to settle here, drawn by the open spaces and forests which still remain.

It took me almost thirty years to return to these hills of home for good after I left them in the late 1960's, and now, as a resident of Halfmoon Valley, near State College in Centre County, I consider every day here as a gift. The name of the valley itself evokes thoughts and images of Indians, witches, wild mountain cats, packs of howling wolves, and the hardy mountaineers who hunted them, but sitting on the deck of my house and looking out over the back of the Bald Eagle Mountains in the distance, I savor the sounds and sights of the country every day. Towards evening, cows moo in the farms across the way as they head for the barn for the night, and day or night the distant sound of a train whistle sometimes carries for miles over the ridges to the north. In the woods beyond my back lawn, squirrels, chipmunks, and deer, including some nice bucks, can often be seen and heard rustling through the leaves in the woods. It is a mixture of atmosphere and tradition that is guaranteed to inspire any writer, and so I continue to write, even though I realize that, in the words of Samuel Johnson, "seldom is any good story wholly true."

Writing these tales is a continuing source of enjoyment and frustration for me. I enjoy seeing the stories appear in printed form once they're written, and I do enjoy writing them, but on the other hand it's often hard to know that I will probably never be given credit for the effort by either historians or folklorists because my subject matter falls into that gray area lying between the two disciplines. I've become more and more convinced that as time goes by I'll probably be labeled a "popularizer" by folklorists since my purpose in writing the books is to do so for non-academics – those who have preserved the tales over the decades by keeping them alive on the currents of oral history. Historians, on the other hand do not consider oral history a reliable source of historical facts, and in this opinion they are most decidedly correct.

In analyzing many of the tales I've collected over the years, I've often been hard-pressed to decide how much is fact and how much is fancy. A good example of this situation is the tale entitled "Sleepless Night in a Haunted House" which appears in Volume I of the series. In that story I preserve an account handed down through several generations of my family, starting with my great-grandfather.

Foster Frazier, my great-grandfather, was a lumberman who claimed to have found a flock of sheep in the second story of an old deserted house somewhere in the Seven Mountains country of Centre and Mifflin Counties during the 1890's. His fellow lumberman regarded the place as haunted until "Foss" decided to sleep there one night and find the source of the haunting. He often recalled this episode for his daughters and grandchildren, relating it as a factual account, not a "tall-tale" that he made up just to entertain people. However, one elderly lady who read the story after my first book was published informed me that she had her doubts about the purported event.

The ninety-year old Centre Countian had been born and raised on a farm during the 1920's, and based on her years of farm life she was sure that although you can prod animals to go up a flight of stairs, you can't get them to go back down once they're up. The simple beasts are too unsure of themselves, she claimed, when it comes to descending steps, and so she thought the sheep in my great-grandfather's story could not have climbed the stairs in the old house and then come back down them again the next morning. I began to think something might have been lost or distorted in my great-grandfather's account as it passed down the generations over the years, but then later another old gentleman living near the small village of Unionville, Centre County, told me about a rundown deserted house which once stood near his farm.

The old mountaineer, who had spent almost his entire life in the shadows of the Allegheny Mountains along a lonely stretch of road known as the Rattlesnake Pike, recalled that years ago a neighboring farmer had a flock of sheep which used a deserted building for shelter. The interesting thing was, he noted, the sheep would enter the building through the front door on the ground floor and then climb steps leading to the second floor. Here they would spend the night, and then come back down the stairs in the morning and go back outside. It was confirmation enough for me that my great-grandfather's tale was probably true after all. Unfortunately, facts like this that provide additional support for, or historical information related to, a tale don't always come to light until after I've already published the account.

Another good example of this type of asynchronous fact finding occurred after I published the story entitled "Indian Summer" in Volume III of the *Pennsylvania Fireside Tales* series. In that account I preserved the Reese family's oral history concerning their ancestor, John Christian Reese, a Hessian mercenary who came to this country with British troops during the Revolutionary War to fight against the American colonists. That was all the information I had about Reese at the time Volume III went to the printer, however additional details surfaced some months later.

Eventually I found out from other Reese family members that their ancestor spelled his name Reis, and that the family name was Anglicized to Reese some years later. Although I had mentioned that John Christian Reis eventually fought for the Colonial cause, I had not known at the time the book went to press that the reason he converted to the patriot side was because he had no choice. According to the other Reese's who I talked to at a later date, the young Hessian was captured by American troops and was given two choices: either fight for the Continental army or be shot by a firing squad. The eighteen-year-old German didn't have to think too long to decide what choice to make.

The choice I continue to make is to write the stories I've collected and hope the public continues to enjoy them. I'm continually amazed by the letters and phone calls I get from ex-Pennsylvanians living all over the United States, including far-away states like Oregon, Texas, and California, wanting to order copies of my books so they can have a touch of home. It is this kind of response that makes my efforts seem worthwhile and which inspires me to continue the task.

In conclusion I'd like to thank my son James for the illustrations which appear in this volume; his talent seems to grow with each drawing he makes. Finally I'd also like to thank those who continue to write or phone me with book orders or a tale they think may be of interest. Please continue to do so (my phone number is 814 692 4842; Address: 143 Cedar Ridge Drive, Port Matilda, Pa. 16870).

WILL - o' - THE -WISP

From time to time the will-o'-the-wisp still appears in the dark hollows and deep woods of the Keystone State. Over the last several centuries there have been many sightings of these strange lights that periodically materialize in our fields and forests, but in recent years such reports have dwindled almost to nothing. Usually found in some of the least-traveled and most isolated sections of the mountains, these flickering blobs of luminescence have been given several different titles by mountain folk over the years. The earthbound variety they've dubbed "foxfire", for reasons unknown to this writer. Then there is the lighter-than-air form of the phenomena, to which the mountaineers have assigned several cognomens, including "will-o'-the-wisps" and "Jack-o'-lanterns". The Pennsylvania Dutch preferred their own name, simply calling them *Erd Lichte* or earth lights [1], but whatever their title, the illuminations always seem to lend a supernatural air to their surroundings when they manifest themselves.

A strange feeling of dread often pervades even entire groups of individuals when they chance upon one of the eerie lights, but the effect is most noticeable to a solitary traveler when he finds himself on a lonely stretch of mountain road at nightfall and happens upon one of these unusual displays. Such witnesses, when asked to describe what they've seen, invariably use the words "ghostly" or "unnatural" to describe the odd phenomena, but those terms, on the other hand, are not altogether surprising.

It's not natural to see a rotting stump glowing in the dark, but this is what happens when "foxfire" illuminates the stump in such a way as to make it appear as though the wood has just been removed from a roaring fire. The material flickers and gleams just like it would if it were covered with glowing coals.

"It just looked like it was on fire!", offered the life-long mountain man who had never lived anywhere except on the farm where he was born. His ancestral home still stands amid some of the wildest and scenic parts of the Seven Mountains, that romantic state forest land that spans the counties of Centre and Mifflin. The old homestead was built in the days when the mountains here teemed with packs of wolves and echoed with the screams of the stately mountain lion. If only the place could talk! What stories would it tell of the old days? But that was why we had come to this house. We had heard that its resident could recount many tales of the olden time, and so it was that he recalled seeing the stump enveloped in foxfire one moonless night while he and his wife were out riding horses after a heavy rain. [2]

However, despite the old story-teller's many interesting experiences in the mountains, and despite the vast store of narratives passed on to him by earlier generations, he had little knowledge of the airborne manifestations called Jack-o'-

lanterns. Even more unnatural looking than their earthbound cousins, aerial versions of the lights take the form of moon-like spheres that bob and weave in unpredictable ways while flickering unsteadily the whole time. The faint-of-heart will want to put as much distance between the lights and themselves as possible, but braver, more curious, souls will elect instead to get a closer look at the unusual displays. This closer inspection will prove easy in the case of foxfire, but surprises are in store for those who try to approach the will-o'-the-wisp, and herein lies the basis for some of the weird legends that usually attach themselves to such lights on those rare occasions when they do appear.

Apparently of unknown origin and purpose, the will-o'-the-wisps have always presented a challenge to those who like to solve nature's mysteries. Almost as though they had some form of intelligence, the dancing orbs of light will never let anyone get close enough to touch them. Despite a person's best efforts, the tenuous balls always manage to float away, remaining just out of reach when someone tries to get near. This decidedly uncanny behavior has led to some novel legends, created by unenlightened souls in the days before science had a chance to study the matter and solve the mystery to everyone's satisfaction.

When they finally conducted careful observations of the light displays, scientists noticed that the mysterious glowing balls usually seem to occur over marshes, where decaying vegetation produces pockets of methane gas that can, under the right conditions, become luminescent. This seems to be the "last word" on the subject, and so experts have labeled the phenomena *ignis fatuus*, or "foolish fire". Most people today have heard this authoritative explanation, and so when they see these unusual displays they know right away that they are nothing more than "swamp gas", and so dismiss them as another of nature's anomalies. Although it's nice to know there is a logical explanation for the will-o'-the-wisps, there is another aspect of the issue that has been pushed aside and almost forgotten in the inexorable advance of science.

It seems that the more knowledgeable and scientifically advanced we become, the less likely we are to remember the simpler times that preceded this present mind-boggling and dollar-mad age. And as we forget those simpler days, we also forget the legends they produced – legends that once served as explanations for natural phenomena that were not explainable within the framework of scientific knowledge that had been constructed at that point in time.

The will-o'-the-wisp is no stranger to other times and places. It's been seen all over the world for centuries, and so has had plenty of opportunity to become heralded in the curious lore and quaint legends of many countries. Cornish miners in England, for example, believed that "a little light jumping around one spot" was a Jack-o'-lantern pinpointing the location of a rich mineral deposit.[3] However, probably the best known of the Jack-o'-lantern tales is the Irish legend that states that Jack-o'-lanterns are the souls of those who are unable to find an abode in either heaven or hell. Too sinful to reside in heaven, and unwelcome in the fiery chambers of Satan's palace because they tricked him when they were still alive, these souls are destined, claims the legend, to wander eternally. And it is a terribly solitary journey, for they wander alone and aimlessly, seen only at night, and then they're only noticed because of the lighted lantern they carry while looking for a place of rest.

In this country the Nanticoke Indians once had their own explanation as to the identity of the Jack-o'-lantern. However, the Nanticokes in Pennsylvania did not consider the lights to be harmless curiosities. To these stalwart sons of the mountains the flickering phantoms of the night were nothing less than evil spirits that "pursue people and bring misfortune". [4] It was an idea that could have come from the white man, but it may have been a notion that originated with the Nanticokes and was eventually adopted by white settlers in Pennsylvania as their own lore. Regardless of where the idea came from, popular belief in the Pennsylvania mountains held that whenever a Jack-o'-lantern appeared it was indeed an ominous sign, and trying to follow one was something only a foolhardy person would do.

"All I heard was that you don't dare follow them if you see them because they'll lead you into some bog or they'll lead you into some destructive place where you'll probably get an injury or you're dead!", recalled the old-time fiddler and folklorist who had heard many such tales in his travels. Taking a sniff of his ever-present snuff, the popular songster elaborated on what he had been told by the old folks he had met in the mountains some seventy years before.

"And so, if anyone saw one, he'd try to go the other way and not even look at it," he continued. "They were afraid of them, and I guess for good reason! I've heard stories about how they'd drop down and hide their faces and shut their ears and eyes, and look up after while. If it was gone, they could resume their journey." [5]

Today there are very few people who would be intimidated and mystified by the strange phosphorescent spheres known as Jack-o'-lanterns. Instead, some folks wonder where they might find them so they can get a closer look.

"I guess they would've called them swamp lights," conjectured the Centre County farmer's wife who had seen them several times when she was a young girl in the first decades of the twentieth century. However, the one she remembered most of all appeared while she and some friends were "coasting" or "sled riding" over snow-crusted fields one winter night in Gregg Township.

"When we were kids, we'd go down to the top of the woods hill there at Paul Zubler's and coast clear up to our place," she fondly recalled. "We'd set up a lantern along and coast the whole livelong evening. And we were coasting, and here we seen this light come from Carl Catherman's garage; and it come out and went around Goodhart's house. And when you looked in the front window you could see out the back and see that light! Why don't we see them now? I just haven't heard a thing about swamp lights for a long long time!" [6]

Being reminded that another fascinating part of Penn's Woods had faded into oblivion was a depressing way to end the evening's conversation, but we had to acknowledge that the lady was correct - there do seem to be fewer and fewer sightings of "swamp lights" as the years go by. The answer as to why this might be the case perhaps lies in the way we seem to be disregarding the natural order of things in this materialistic era. We cut down our forests, run new highways roughshod over prime woodlands and farms, and shamelessly pollute our waters, all in the quest for bigger profits while denying the effect it will have on our grandchildren's quality of life. Will-o'-the-wisps, seemingly sensing our disrespect and disregard for the things that they held most dear, have perhaps decided they can no longer bear to see what's being done to their surroundings.

There is, on the other hand, a more positive explanation that can be offered as to the relative scarcity of swamp light reports. It just might be that science, in its forward progression, has indeed explained the phenomenon to most peoples' satisfaction so that the shimmering spheres don't even arouse our curiosities any more. Certainly a more pleasant explanation than the idea that we're irreparably destroying our planet, but it still contains the same seeds of disregard for the wonders of nature around us. It would seem, however, that of the two postulations the second idea is the less defensible. Surely most of us would want to get a closer look at the strange lights if we encountered one. For wherever they appear they do create a sensation, just like the Will-o'-the-Wisp that appeared in Mifflin County almost forty years ago.

Reports of a ghostly light that could be seen in the mountains back of McVeytown during the early 1960's attracted a host of curious onlookers, adults and teenagers alike, to that little community along the waters of the "Blue Juniata". In fact, people in all of Mifflin County's "river towns" heard stories of the McVeytown sightings for a period of several months, but it was McVeytown where the most graphic descriptions were overheard and where directions to the "ghost light" were most readily obtained. Teenagers in search of thrills particularly liked to seek out the light in the foothills of Jacks Mountain. Sometimes their nocturnal visits were rewarded with a sighting, other times not, but that did not stop them from coming, and from wondering if any of the legends about the light were true.

It's doubtful that most of the youthful visitors looking for the ghost light knew much about the history of either the mountain near where it appeared or of the little town in the shadows below. Such facts are unimportant to those who are seeking ghosts, and so none of the youngsters would have been thinking historical thoughts. Not the type of details to be bothered with on a ghost hunt. In their excitement, none of the thrill seekers probably knew or recalled that the familiar mountain town they had just passed through was named Waynesburg before it became McVeytown, but some of them might have wondered if the Jack of Jacks Mountain and the Jack of the Jack-o'-lantern were one-in- the-same person.

Jacks Mountain does seem to be one of those places that has always been a favorite haunting ground for "spooks", and for those who wish to discover more about Jacks Mountain, the history of its name, and another one of its ghosts, they can read the author's story entitled "Jack's Narrows" which appeared in the second volume of this series. But despite its reputation as a spectral playground, Jacks Mountain did not lend its name to the Jack-o'-lantern which appeared in the mountain's foothills above McVeytown. In fact the ghostly light is known by entirely different names, depending on which version of the legend about it you might hear.

There seem to be many renditions of the tale. In some cases there are no names at all mentioned in the telling of the ghost-light story. However, more specific details are offered in two of the most popular accounts, including names and dates. In the one case the light is said to be "John Horning's lantern"; in the other, the light is simply referred to as "Irving's ghost". The legend of John Horning and his lantern will be explored in the next chapter in this volume. In this essay we'll tell the story of Irving's ghost. After digesting the various accounts, readers can decide for themselves which legend, if any, might contain kernels of truth that have been hiding for decades in these remnants of a bygone day.

"Irving", it is said, was a slave belonging to a local farmer around the time of the Civil War. The black man was apparently not attuned to the tenor of this turbulent period, or he would not have done what the legend purports. Irving, it seems, had admired his "master's" finer things for years. Then one day the urge to own jewels or fine paintings of his own overwhelmed the man's better instincts, and he carried some of the most prized pieces away, with apparently no idea where he would go or what he would do with them. In an attempt to buy some time, the desperate man decided to hide his ill-gotten gains in the woods along a field that adjoins the little rise known today as Irwin's Hill (named after a man named Irwin, who was the pioneer settler in that section).

It must have given the thief some pleasure from time to time to sneak up to his hidden treasure and admire it, but the legend states that eventually the county sheriff pinned the crime on Irving and came after him one day. Assuming they would hang him if captured, Irving made one last trip to the place where he had stashed his loot. In an old building that was standing nearby, the frightened desperado found a rope and hanged himself.

Decades passed before the disjointed particles of Irving's spirit could coalesce into a manifestation that could be seen in the form of the McVeytown ghost light, but it was Irving's ghost, claims this legend, that accounts for the light that sometimes could be seen bobbing and weaving through the trees beside the field.[7]

Today all that is left of the woods where Irving is said to have hidden his treasure is a small plot of forest and an adjacent row of trees along the top of the hill where the light was often seen. Now just a tangle of wild grape vines and thickets of blackberry bushes, this mini-wilderness seems impenetrable, even for a Jack-o'-lantern. In fact, the dense undergrowth appears to have discouraged the light's visits lately since it has not appeared in recent years.

"I haven't seen it in the ten years I've lived here," claims a local resident who lives in a house with a perfect view of the haunted tree line. We were ready to accept this as the last word on the matter until the same individual noted that some strange things have happened in his house since he moved there. Loud footsteps have been heard in parts of the house where no human was walking at the time. Another time, the man came home to find his garage all cleaned up. Thinking his wife had done him a favor, he and she were both shocked when they realized neither one had performed the task.[8]

Although disquieting, the ghostly visitor, it that's what it was, seems friendly enough, and even helpful at times. One might even say that Irving's ghost had turned over a new leaf. Tired of floating aimlessly as a ball of phosphorescent nothingness, the remorseful spirit may now be trying to atone for wrongs done while in human form. On the other hand, there is another version of the tale that readers may want to peruse before deciding one way or another on this weighty matter. The next story, entitled "The Ghostly Lantern", has more to say about the strange ghost light of Irwin's Hill.

THE GHOSTLY LANTERN

Some people would say that the privilege of seeing a ghost is a rare event; one which is experienced by only a lucky few who are either thrilled and amazed or frightened out of their wits by the encounter. Others are content just to read about revenants, thinking that it's far better to be scared "second-hand" rather than feel an apparition's icy breath on the back of their own neck. Then there are those who don't believe in such things unless they see them for themselves. These skeptics contend that "spooks" were never more than fanciful products of fairytales from an earlier time, and anyway, they say, science has replaced the old order of thinking; if there were any such things as ghosts, they were "laid" a long time ago. However, it seems some of these spectral visitors haven't found out yet that they no longer exist. New wraiths seem to pop up all the time, if legends are to be believed, and many of the older ghosts still promenade at night, hauntingly laughing at those who dare to proclaim them extinct.

One such playful specter surfaced about forty years ago on Irwin's Hill above the little community of McVeytown, creating quite a stir in Mifflin and surrounding counties. While some said the so-called ghost was nothing more than a "will-o'-the-wisp", or a "Jack-o-lantern", others weren't so sure. This specter was, they could claim, just one more among many that had surfaced in the Juniata Valley over the years. And, furthermore, they might note, McVeytown does sit beside the brooding countenance of Jacks Mountain, which, it might be said, is no stranger to visitors from the realms of the spirit world. And at least one early historian of the Juniata region would support such claims.

Uriah J. Jones, that somewhat discredited author of *History of the Early Settlement of the Juniata Valley*, notes in his interesting account that the first settlers in the hollows and forests in and around Jacks Mountain told and retold stories about a specter that was said to appear at the head of Jack's spring, believing it to be the spirit of the notorious "Black Hunter". The Black Hunter, variously known as Captain Jack, the Black Rifle, or the Wild Hunter of the Juniata, formed the basis for many colorful tales and accounts along the waters of the Juniata in the mid-1700's. Most of these folk tales are now forgotten, and the ghost of Captain Jack was laid to rest with them, but his memory will endure as long as the Juniata Valley mountains he was said to roam.

Some interesting accounts of Captain Jack can still be heard today, but historians now agree that the man appears to be nothing more than a myth. Nonetheless, the legends about the Black Hunter's ghost may still be causing people to wonder just how many other lesser-known phantoms have established their earthly residences in the wild recesses of the Juniata Valley. In fact other legends occasionally do come to light intimating that the

Black Hunter's ghost would not be alone if it were still roaming about the stately pines and along the rhododendron-lined streams of Jacks Mountain.

Although there are probably many others in and around the Juniata Valley that could be mentioned, most notably that of Chief Logan's ghost near Reedsville (a story which will be included in a future volume of *Fireside Tales*), Captain Jack's most recent spectral companion seems to be the Jack-o'-lantern some called Irving's ghost. Said to be the spirit of a black thief who hanged himself in the foothills of Jacks Mountain around the time of the Civil War, this luminous ball of light appeared near Irwin's Hill above McVeytown, Mifflin County, in the early 1960's, drawing nightly crowds who came to see the unusual display. However, the floating orb seemed to enjoy teasing the onlookers, sometimes showing up on a nightly basis, and then not appearing again for weeks. This irregularity led to doubts in some peoples' minds as to the very existence of the glowing sphere, but these doubters were chiefly those who took the trouble to make the trip up the mountain, spend hours watching, and see only moonbeams and shadows.

Doubts and confusion always seemed to arise when discussions about the light took place. Not only were there people who refused to believe in the possibility of such odd displays, but even many of those who saw it were uncertain as to its origins. There were those who accepted the scientific explanations and wrote it off as "swamp gas" or car lights, but those theories didn't satisfy the believers, who argued that there was only one dull light rather than two shiny ones, and that the single light didn't dissipate like swamp gas would. But despite their convictions, the believers still had to decide on another matter, and that was which legend about the Jack-o-lantern was the true one. Besides the story about the ghost of the black thief, there were at least three other accounts about how the "haunt" on the hill came to be there in the first place, and all three had their proponents.

Women may have been more disposed to believe in the first legend, which claimed that the unpredictable display on Irwin's Hill was the ghost of a woman hunting her lost dog.

"It was a woman lookin' for her dog," recalled the valley native. "Her dad gave her a coon dog for her birthday. She trained the dog, and they were out huntin' one night, and the dog never come back. She heard him barkin' and carryin' on, and she spent all night lookin' for it; and all night the next night lookin' for it. Third night, you know, she went out again, and she never come back! So they never found the dog. She's out lookin' for her dog." [1]

Others who saw the ethereal light may have decided that its origins were best explained by the legend about the local farmer who kept a herd of cows as his pets.

"The story was that a farmer was really attached to his cows, like family members, and someone killed them as a prank," explained one young man who had seen the shimmering ball as it wound its way through the line of trees it seemed to call home.

"He would go out every night with a lantern to bring the cows in from the field," continued the young storyteller. "And he went out this one night and found all the cows dead, and went insane. Even after the carcasses were taken away, he would go out with a lantern every night, thinking the cows were still there. And when he died he supposedly kept going out, trying to find the cows." [2]

A third, more detailed, account that attempts to offer an explanation for the uncanny display also claims that the light is that of a ghostly lantern. In this case the ghost carrying the lantern is said to be the vapory essence of another farmer who, when in human form, also went out one night looking for his cattle.

This story relates that sometime in the 1930's, when electricity had not yet found its way into the remoter sections of the mountains, a man named John Horning had to go out after supper looking for his cows. They had not come home at sunset, and so now that it was dark the concerned farmer lit a lantern and went out into the night to search for the prodigal animals. Horning's lantern, so it is said, could be seen weaving its way through the trees in the woods next to Irwin's Hill. It is not known whether the farmer ever found his cows, but the legend says he did find his wife in the arms of her lover there in the woods. Overcome with rage, Horning went berserk and killed his wife and her paramour on the spot. Now, it seems, on certain nights of the year when the night winds sigh in the blackberry thickets and whistle through the tangles of wild grape vines that choke the haunted tree line on Irwin's Hill, the faint glow of John Horning's lantern can be seen winding its way through the trees. It is Horning's restless spirit, so the legend implies, that must eternally patrol the spot where the farmer's wife and her lover were so brutally murdered. [3]

Those inclined to analyze these types of stories in a no-nonsense methodical sort of way would agree that it would be very difficult to uncover historical facts that might support a ghost story like this one. It would take a lot of "digging" to determine if a man named John Horning once lived at Irwin's Hill and murdered his wife, but the fact is there are still quite a few Horning's that live in the area. There are Hornings in Lewistown, some in Thompsontown, and still others in Mifflintown, but, even though their presence there today does indicate there could have once been a Horning named John who was the same John Horning of the legend, it doesn't prove it. In that regard then, the ghostly light still remains a mystery to anyone who wants to believe the old account. And the believers are those who have seen the light, particularly people who have had the most frightening experiences with it.

Among those who have had some hair-raising encounters with the ghost light are the group of teenagers who, in the 1960's, took a ride up to Irwin's Hill one night just to see if they could see the "ghost" and communicate with it in some way. It was to be a way to be frightened and entertained at the same time, but the party of thrill seekers became more and more disappointed as they waited and waited without seeing the hoped-for apparition.

In order to entertain the group, even though they'd all heard the account before, one of the boys retold the legend of the old farmer who had found his pet cows slaughtered. He retold the episode in all its gory details, embellishing it more than it had been embellished before, hoping to scare the young ladies. The young raconteur ended the story by reminding them all that it was that same old farmer's ghost, and its ghostly lantern, that haunted the tree line, destined to search for his cows forever. Desiring even greater thrills, someone then suggested that they all run through the field and up to the haunted woods, but one of the more timid girls was reluctant to make such a bold move.

Hundreds of fireflies seemed to be out in the field that night and their continuous illuminations reminded her of a thousand little eyes. As she watched the tiny blinking lights, she began to get the uneasy feeling that someone or some thing was watching her. Torn between joining the rest or staying behind in the car by herself, she decided to join the group rather than risk having the light come into the car with her.

Hand in hand, the entire party ran through the field, screaming louder and louder as they got closer and closer to the haunted forest. Then, before they reached their objective, several people tripped, causing others to fall also. Those who had fallen first stood up, and, in the midst of the confusion and consternation, one of them found the "stone" they had stumbled over. Pandemonium broke out among the girls in the group when they realized the "stone" was a cow's skull.

Screaming and yelling, the frightened ghost hunters ran all the way back to the car, but one of the bolder young men carried the cow's skull back with him. Placing it on the hood of the automobile, he and the other boys had a good laugh as they watched the terrified girls struggling wildly to get into the vehicle. Their laughter was short-lived. At that moment the light appeared in the woods. However, this night it didn't stay there. Slowly and silently, as if guided by some intelligent hand, the flickering ball began moving toward the car. Frightened beyond belief, the entire party piled into the auto, and, as one of the girls was later to say, they "screeched out of there – never to return again!" [4]

Undeterred by experiences like that of the teens who had found the cow's skull and then saw the ghostly lantern, another party of thrill-seeking young people went up to Irwin's Hill in 1972. They, too, wanted to see the ghost, "Irvin's ghost", as it was then called by the teenage crowd.

It was an October night, recalled as sometime "just before hunting season", and three young daredevils decided to see if they could conjure up the lonely ghost that everyone had been talking about. The driver of the car had recently gotten his driver's license, and he wanted to do something exciting, so he took two friends along up to Irwin's Hill. After parking the car at the foot of the road leading up to the trees where the light would surface, the driver and his friends settled down to await events.

Soon the light appeared, as if it had an appointment to keep, and slowly the faintly luminescent ball began moving through the trees at the top of the hill. It was later remembered as a "glowing light that flickered; about waist high" and looking "just like a lantern". The glowing ball never strayed from its course, weaving in and out among the trees that now stood where old fence posts and a fence once enclosed a farmer's field.

Eventually the lantern-like orb reached the point in the old fence line where the trees had been cut away for the road to pass through. Knowing that the light, if it followed its past patterns, would cross the road and then shortly disappear into the adjoining woods, the impetuous new driver decided he would have some fun with the 22 rifle he'd brought along.

The young marksman took careful aim at the shimmering yellow ball that was now in the middle of the road, and he slowly pulled the trigger. Instead of a loud explosion, the boys only heard a sharp click as the gun's hammer landed squarely on the live shell in the firing chamber. Impatiently the rifleman ejected the defective shell and pumped another cartridge into the firing position. Once again he took careful aim and slowly pulled the trigger, only to hear the same clicking sound as before. A third time a shot was attempted, but it, too, proved to be a dud.

By this time the light had deviated from its normal path, turning and heading for the car. It continued on its course, but at the last minute it veered off and came to a silent rest behind the parked vehicle. Still somewhat awestruck, the anxious teens stood beside the auto and wondered what to do next. There was nothing in the field except the light, the boys who had shot at it, and their automobile, and not a sound broke the stillness of the uncanny confrontation. Not even the slightest breeze was stirring the dried weeds that were still standing in the open field, and the silence was unnerving. Just then a loud snapping or cracking sound, like that of a tree splitting in half, came from the middle of the clearing.

It was all the incentive the boys needed to seek the relative safety of the car. "We jumped in the car and spun around and shined the headlights up into the field," recalled the driver in calmer tones than he would have used on that night. "There was absolutely, positively, no trees – there was nothing up in there!"

The boys decided that further investigation was not a good idea, agreeing that they'd had enough ghost hunting for one night. Without much discussion they "flew down over the hill and went home!" [5] They would no doubt agree with others who had challenged the light and lost that it was better to run and live to see another day than to stand and fight the ghostly lantern.

Footnote:

There are others who say that the ball of light was first seen up on Irwin's Hill , rather than along the tree line that stands on the other side of the field that lies next to the hill. They also say that if anyone wants to claim that the light is a ghost, then they should consider that it might be the spirit of old Irwin himself . These folks contend that Irwin's wife committed suicide by hanging herself from the sturdy limb of a tree on the hill that was named after the first family to settle here. According to this tale, the old settler found his wife hanging from the tree and buried her near it. Too distraught to face life alone, the bereaved husband hanged himself from the same tree. Although the woods on top of the hill is now being developed, there are still sections that are densely overgrown. It is said that somewhere in this deep dark woods are the tombstones that mark the final resting place of the last Irwins of Irwin's hill. [6]

On Irwin's Hill

(Row of trees and field where the ghostly lantern was seen)

Near McVeytown, Mifflin County

PUNXSUTAWNEY

People up in Jefferson County don't seek publicity anymore than the average person, but whether they like it or not, every February second their small city of Punxsutawney becomes the center of national attention. Even though its name alone might be enough to make the borough somewhat of a tourist curiosity, it's the town's unusual resident that causes such a stir. Formerly an occupant of a subterranean dwelling up on top of nearby Gobbler's Knob, where his illustrious ancestors first settled, the celebrity now lives in comfort in the town's Civic Center. The name of this famous resident is Phil. He has no last name, but he really doesn't need one. Those who talk about him, public and press alike, just call him "Punxsutawney Phil", and that's enough of a handle for most people to recognize who they're talking about.

There is a reason for this notoriety, and it doesn't originate from any great heroic deeds that were performed or from any notorious ones either. Phil's whole claim to fame rests in his touted ability to predict if there will be six more weeks of winter following February second or whether spring will arrive in a matter of several weeks thereafter. He accomplishes this using very simple procedures, and without the aid of expensive and intricate scientific instruments. In fact, it's all done by means of his shadow. If he sees it, then there will be six more weeks of winter, but if he doesn't, then spring is just around the corner.

In reality, Phil probably doesn't care one way or the other. You see, Phil is a groundhog, and February second is Groundhog Day. It is actually the Punxsy Groundhog Club that decides whether Phil sees his shadow or not, and they've been in the business since 1884. For almost one-hundred years no one questioned the validity of the club's predictions, but eventually statisticians, those inveterate analyzers of numbers and trends, took it upon themselves to look at the data. Flying in the face of time-honored tradition, they concluded that Phil's accuracy is highly exaggerated; his track record just doesn't stand up to the hard, cold, numbers of reality.

Such overwhelming evidence would be enough to discourage even the most ardent believers, but there are still those who like to support their local hero. Old beliefs "die hard", and perhaps this one is such an ancient idea that it's difficult for the human race to discount it altogether.

There are those who claim the roots underlying the groundhog legend reach all the way back to the ancient Greeks, who believed, according to some sources, that an animal's shadow was its soul blackened by last year's sins. These same ancients also thought that the only way the animal's soul could be purified was through a long winter hibernation. When it awoke in the spring and emerged from its winter quarters, the animal would see its shadow if its winter sleep hadn't been long enough for a thorough cleansing of the soul. I've not been able to verify that claim, but whether it was the Greeks or some other race who laid the foundations for the groundhog legend, the belief did find its way around the world, settling most notably in America and in England.

In England the legend of the groundhog's weather wisdom is connected to the yearly milestone known as Candlemas, which also falls on February second. This popular holy day is said to date back to the fourth century, its foundations traceable to the birth of Christ, but over the years the celebration of the "candle mass" has also become associated with the following familiar idea:

"If Candlemas be fair and bright,
Come, winter, have another flight
If Candlemas bring clouds and rain,
Go, winter, and come not again". [1]

Although in America these same ideas have not been set down in poetical form, they have persisted, regardless of doubts about the origins of the belief and its utility. As a result, Punxsutawney Phil has maintained his reputation. In fact, just like the highly-touted quick draw artists of the Old West, there's always someone gunning for him; trying to outdo him. Phil has his competitors, and the rivalry is not the most amiable one. Each of the groundhogs has his following, and each is held to be the true predictor of spring weather; all other woodchuck weather prophets except the local prognosticator are considered lowly imposters.

Among those who claim their groundhog is the one and only true seer is the Slumbering Groundhog Lodge in Lancaster County. Here every February second, on the banks of Puddleduck Creek near the town of Quarryville, members of the Slumbering Lodge congregate to see what their Octorora Orphie has predicted. With the tension in the air building minute by minute, the men gather at the business end of a manure spreader and watch their leader mount the unusual speaking platform to announce whether or not Orphie has seen his shadow. However, Orphie is nothing but a poor imposter, according to Punxsutawney Phil's followers, because, unlike Phil, Orphie is stuffed. He's as dead as a doornail, and he's as incapable of seeing his shadow as he is of whistling like he did when he was a real live "whistle pig"!

As a live model, Punxsutawney Phil can always say he's not a "dummy" like his challenger, but in any case it doesn't seem to matter to the public. The whole business is interesting enough to attract national press coverage every year, and it will probably stay that way as long as there is a Groundhog Day. However, the interest in Punxsutawney Phil does seem to have overshadowed the story behind his unusual name. Most people hardly give it a second thought anymore, but the town is named after a Delaware Indian village that in pioneer days stood on the same site. However, what is even less well known is the legend about the place; a tale that says an Indian once lived here who, in his own way, created as much excitement as Punxsutawney Phil does today.

When the first white men first penetrated into the depths of what is now Jefferson County, they found it to be an inhospitable place. These men were the Moravian missionaries whose life work was to bring the Gospel to the Indians, and these bearers of God's holy word often kept daily journals of their experiences. One of these fearless and dedicated men, who was accustomed to encountering all the discomforts and hardships the Pennsylvania wilderness had to offer, found the Punxsutawney area to be particularly inhospitable. Describing it as an almost impassible swamp overgrown with thorn bushes, he mentions how the huge thorns "tore our clothes and flesh, both hands and face to a bad degree", and bemoans the fact that "we had such a road all day." [2]

But despite the hostile environment, the Indians found Punxsutawney to be a place where they could sustain a village. According to historical accounts, the Delaware maintained a town here for centuries, seemingly unconcerned about the swampy ground and the fact that it was a fertile breeding ground for mosquitoes and those infernal pests known as sand-flies. Unable to resort to effective insect repellents like we have today, the Indians used other means to protect themselves from the aggressive insects that plagued the area, the most common method being smearing of animal grease over the exposed parts of their bodies. However, even these measures sometimes failed to ward off the worst attackers, the almost invisible hellions the Delaware called *ponkis* and the white man would later call gnats or sand-flies.

The pests were so awful that the Indians thought they had to be creations of some demon rather than of their Great Spirit. Why else, so they reasoned, would the bites of these tiny insects be as "hot as sparks of fire " or burn like "hot ashes"? [3]

So unbelievably vicious were these infernal nuisances that extraordinary Moravian missionary John Ettwein even mentions them in one of his journals. Born in the Schwarzwald of Germany in 1712, Ettwein never experienced anything in Germany's Black Forest like the "ponkies" of Punxsutawney. Describing them as "vermin", Ettwein notes they were "a plague to man and beast, both day and night". On some occasions they were so thick that the bishop could not hold church services, and on one particular night they were so oppressive that a herd of cattle tried to squeeze into the missionaries' camp, seeking to "escape their persecutors in the smoke of the fires." [3]

Ettwein also claims that the name the Indians gave to this infernal place was *Ponksutenink*, or "town of the ponkis". The Delaware also had a quaint legend about the swamp, which they passed on to the dedicated missionary. It is this curious tale that explains why the Delaware once believed their ancestors avoided this place like it was the proverbial entrance to the underworld. [3]

According to the legend the Indians told the missionaries, there had once been a time, somewhere in the distant past, when an old hermit lived by the swamp. The Indians never mentioned which tribe the recluse might have belonged to, probably because they never knew. In fact, the legend would indicate that no one ever got close enough to find out.

In those days, "long time ago", as the Indians would say, it seems there were no *ponkis* here to annoy trespassers and chase them away. If there had been hoards of biting insects in this marshland, they would have been a delight to the old Indian, who hated interlopers of any kind. He seemed to hold a special grudge against anyone who dared to hunt on the real estate he seemed to think was his and his alone, and in order to discourage hunters he used his powers as a sorcerer to change himself into grotesque and frightful shapes in order to scare them off. If this failed, then he was not adverse to murdering those who wandered into his territory and robbing them of any pelts and skins they might be carrying.

The miscreant got away with his foul crimes for many years, until one day a more powerful sorcerer was found who was able to kill the hated hermit. Taking no chances, the Indians decided they would burn the evil man's body so he could not use powerful magic to bring himself back to life. Placing the dead man on a high funeral pyre, the Indians watched gleefully as the flames consumed the corpse and the winds scattered the sparks and ashes into the nearby swamp.

Eventually, and the legend doesn't say how long it took, the Indians began to notice that the swamp was now infested with small, almost invisible, insects whose bites stung like hot sparks from a blazing fire. The name they chose for the bugs reflected their belief that the pests were the still-living sparks and hot ashes that came from the detested sorcerer's funeral pyre. The Delaware called the insects *ponkis,* which the white man would later verbalize as ponkies or "punkies". The name meant "living dust and ashes". [3]

Historical Notes:

The Moravian missionaries who first came to the swampland that is now present-day Punxsutawney called the place "Ashtown", probably basing the name on the Indian legend. The earliest white settlers here, perhaps ignorant of the Indian's name, placed their own title upon the land. Impressed by the swarms of gnats that seemed to plague them, both by day and by night, the whites called the territory "Gnattown". [4]

Descriptions of Indian war dances that have come down to us from those same Moravian missionaries indicate that grotesque expressions and postures were an integral part of the Indians' tactics when confronting an enemy. They would, during their war dances, "make wild leaps" and "utter weird cries" while clicking their teeth and snapping their fingers in an attempt to show how they would confront such an enemy. [5] The object of such posturing was, noted another missionary, "to excel each other by their terrific looks and gestures", hoping to "strike terror in the beholders". [6]

Native American ceremonial rites and costumes could be unnerving to the uninitiated. One unsuspecting Moravian brother was walking through a Delaware Indian village with its chief one day, and suddenly was confronted by the medicine man, dressed to look like a horned bear, So appalling was the shaman's performance that the missionary was convinced that the thing was a real animal.

"I was so frightened," he recalled, "that I flew immediately to other other side of the chief, who observing my agitation and the quick strides I made, asked me what was the matter, and what I thought is was I saw before me".

The missionary replied that he thought it was a bear or some other type of vicious animal, and confessed he didn't have any idea what was inside, noting it was something "not to be looked at by everybody". [7]

This type of reaction was just the kind of effect the old Indian hermit at Punxsutawney, if he ever did exist, would have hoped for when he appeared in his "frightful shapes" to scare trespassers away. All he may have needed was a horrifying costume and the right gestures to achieve his goals. On the other hand, perhaps the Indians had an entire mythology of their own, which included a character like Proteus of Greek myths, who could change his shape and appearance at will in order to avoid capture. In any case the idea was not just confined to Punxsutawney, because the legends of Luzerne County mention "Indian Toby" who lived in a cave near Larksville. Old Toby, it was said, hated intruders too, and tried to frighten them away with "weird sights and sounds". [8] Then, too, vague and unsubstantiated legendary accounts in Clearfield County describe a sorcerer much like the one at Punxsutawney, saying that because of him the Indians named that place "no one tarries here willingly". [9]

Eventually neither the punkies nor anti-social Indian sorcerers were able to keep white intruders from claiming what was once a no-man's land. In the process, the legends about the Indian sorcerer at Punxsutawney were effaced as completely as the punkies that were once so prevalent at this same place. However, this means that Punxsutawney Phil's days of glory are assured. He has been, and probably will remain for some time, Punxsutawney's greatest celebrity.

The Weather Prophet

(Punxsutawney Phil look-alike courtesy of Cohick's Trading Post, Salladasburg, Lycoming County. Here, on a high dusty shelf in the back of the store, this nameless whistle pig sits with other stuffed creatures, perhaps dreaming of days long ago when he could see his own shadow.)

A TROPHY BUCK

"I can show you some nice horns," declared the veteran Clinton County Nimrod whose hunting experiences spanned a period of almost eighty years. "We had some good old hunters here in this little town when I was a kid," continued the old farmer. "Roy Smull, the Walizers (Perry, Dick, and Jim), Ed Reish from Salona, and my uncle Bill Jones. Our gang here in Mackeyville was the first to kill six deer in a season. I got some nice horns, but at that time we had horns; when they were four and five inches around the beams! You don't see those kind anymore. I don't know what's the matter. Now you'll get an eight point, and he'll have little points like your little finger! It just isn't huntin' anymore." [1]

Several of us were at Elmwood Farms in Mackeyville, visiting Clifford Vonada, the town's oldest resident, and after hearing him talk about his trophies of the chase we told him we'd be delighted if he would show them to us.

"I've got some upstairs in the house, and I've got more in the garage outside," exclaimed the aged hunter. "Did you ever see a shovel buck?," he asked, but we admitted we were at a loss as to what he was talking about. Jovially he explained that a shovel buck was a deer whose antlers were palmated, or flattened out. We told him we'd never seen such a specimen and would very much like to get a picture, whereupon we were escorted to the old shed outside.

As we walked up to the frame building whose wooden siding was blackened with age, we seemed to enter another world. In the yard stood an old cast iron hitching post with an iron ring, where many fine horses must have waited patiently for their riders under the shadows created by the stately elm trees that apparently once grew here. Decorating the top of the post was a likeness of a horse's head, watching silently over the premises and serving as a reminder of a less-hurried era when the automobile had not yet disturbed the tranquility of this peaceful countryside and the mountains beyond.

A further relic of those halcyon times was displayed on one wall on the outside of the old shed. Hanging from a single nail, and standing out in stark contrast to the slate gray siding of the building, was a white granite drinking cup, the kind that was used to quench many a farm hand's parched throat with ice cold well water during hot summer days. It was an antique that made us wonder what other links with the past we might find inside the shed once we entered this weather-beaten survivor of another age.

Inside the wooden building were even more mementos of days gone by. Old horseshoes, and tools adorned the walls, as well as other relics from the times when back-breaking manual labor was the lot of the husbandman. We looked upon the display with admiration, but as our eyes became accustomed to the dimly lit interior, we soon noticed that the most prominent decorations on the walls were many sets of antlers, from the deer the old man had killed over the years. He had "laid low" some nice six and eight "point" specimens in his time, but displayed in the most prominent place in the building, at the top of the wall facing the door as you enter, were the antlers of the "shovel buck". As I snapped picture after picture of the rare souvenir, I wondered how many others like it had ever been taken anywhere else in the mountains of Pennsylvania.

From the days when the Pennsylvania woods was still a virgin forest, described by one colorful poet as a place as "lonely and enchanted as e'er beneath a waning moon was haunted," [2] until today, the horns of a magnificent buck have always been one of the most sought-after prizes of the serious hunter. With some antlers having as many as fifteen or more "points", or prongs, sprouting off the main stems, it is not surprising that these mementos of the chase stand out better on the walls of a trophy room than any others. Little wonder it is then that hunters here in Pennsylvania, and in other places as well, love to recount the tales of how the big ones got away or how they fell to the unerring aim of a lucky hunter who happened to be in the right place at the right time. However, on rare occasions it seems it doesn't even take a lot of effort or a well-aimed shot to get that special trophy.

During their most temperamental season, the summer months of July and August, male deer have been known to fight one another to the death. During this period the bucks are apt to quarrel at the least provocation, and when a fight begins it is a desperate one, with no quarter offered by either contestant. Philip Tome, noted hunter and pioneer of the West Branch country, once came across two such combatants on a mountain in Clinton County. The two bucks were engaged in a terrific struggle and their antlers were locked. Completely oblivious to anything else around them, except perhaps for the doe that was standing nearby, the two unlucky stags and the doe all fell victim to the rifleman's bullets.

On at least two other occasions the old hunter didn't even have to waste his ammunition to collect several nice sets of antlers. Once when hunting in the mountains along Pine Creek, Tome found two bucks lying dead, "each bearing the fatal marks of the other's antlers". On another outing he found one dying buck "his antlers interlocked with those of another, already dead." [3]

Such scenes were also once reported in Susquehanna County, where pioneer hunter Daniel Spencer found a starving buck whose horns were permanently interlocked with those of another. The second buck had died from either starvation or from wounds inflicted by the horns of the first deer. The survivor had no other choice but to drag around his victim until he "had become a mere skeleton" and was barely alive himself. [4]

Interlocked antlers aren't always the only kind that are sometimes there for the taking. Meshach Browning, born in 1781, and who could easily be called the "Daniel Boone of the southern Alleghenies", lived a life that was filled with many hunting exploits in pursuit of the panther, the wolf, and the white-tailed deer. During his forty-four years of hunting, Browning claimed that it was not unusual to find antlers where the bucks had dropped them. Every winter the horns apparently freeze, and then in several weeks fall off. Lucky hunters will sometimes find them "with a quantity of hair attached". [5]

Although luck plays a part when a hunter finally gets the big set of antlers he has hoped for, sheer grit, clever tactics, and ragged determination are usually the deciding factors between failure and success. And when it comes to rare courage and clever tactics, there's probably no better case on record than that of a heroine in early nineteenth century Susquehanna County. Seeing her brother-in-law desperately struggling with a wounded buck one day, the young lady realized that if he lost his grip on the deer's antlers he could be severely gouged. Without a moment's hesitation, the quick-witted girl unwound her long-webbed garters, and "speedily succeeded" in binding the deer's legs until a neighbor arrived and killed the animal. [6]

There are some bucks that seem to be just as cunning and clever as the humans who hunt them. These are the stags that grow old enough to develop the biggest sets of antlers, or "racks", in the hunter's vernacular, and who seem to survive despite the many gunners who try to track them down year after year. During the 1800's and early 1900's some of these seemingly invincible bucks were even given nicknames by their pursuers. At least that was the case for one such buck that led an apparently charmed life in Centre and Mifflin Counties during that time period.

For about a decade, between 1910 and 1920, a huge buck was reported to be roaming the wilds of the northern Seven Mountains country. Every year there would be sightings of the stag with the big set of antlers, and every year hunters from far and wide would try to bring him down. However, all attempts to do so always failed, and there were many frustrated trophy seekers as a result. The buck's uncanny ability to stay alive seemed to surprise a lot of people, and many discussions took place as to why he led such a charmed life.

There seemed to be only one plausible explanation: there were really several large bucks that people were mistaking for the same one year after year. However, the hunters that had tracked the magnificent stag knew this was not true because the wily buck had a deformed hoof which left an unmistakable imprint on the forest floor.

Since the most reasonable explanation for the buck's charmed life was obviously not the true one, it probably seemed to most folks that consideration of other rational theories was pointless. It was one of those unsolvable mysteries that popped up occasionally and one which at least some felt could only be explained by supernatural considerations.

About that time there was a person living in the area who was believed to be a powerful wizard. Emanuel Breon, it was said, could put a spell on a buck, or on any other wild animal for that matter, so that it could not be killed by a hunter's bullets. The old hex lived somewhere near the Synagogue Gap, that wild defile that connects Georges and Decker Valleys in Centre County, and that was where the big buck that had seemed immortal for almost a decade was most often seen. The evidence seemed to fall in place, and without any other reasonable explanations to account for the stag's invincibility, people accepted the supernatural one: "Man" Breon had "hexed" the buck so it couldn't be shot by anyone. From that time on the stag became known as "Man's buck".

The old hart did seem to be a phantom. Very few people ever had the privilege of seeing Man's buck, and even fewer had the opportunity to take a shot at him. Jared B. Ripka, old time lumberman of Spring Mills, Centre County, recalled in 1971 how one day, almost seventy years earlier, he almost got his chance.

"J B", as the old timer preferred to be addressed, remembered very vividly the day he was over near the Synagogue Gap cutting down trees on George Breon's farm. He was working in a heavily lumbered area where a lot of chestnut trees had been cut.

"The stumps were still fresh looking since chestnut timber doesn't rot," explained the old woodsman.

"I had just filled my pipe, and then found I didn't have any matches," he continued.

"I thought to myself that this might be a long day if I didn't have my pipe to help pass the time. I was standing at the top of several trees that had been cut, and they were lying with their bases pointing down the mountain, so I laid down my ax and walked down to the base of one of the trees where I had left my hunting coat. When I got there I looked in my pockets for matches, but couldn't find any. Just then I heard hunting horns."

The noise seemed to be coming from on top of a knob in the Synagogue Gap, and J B, hunter that he was, never gave the sounds another thought. Disappointed at finding no matches, the frustrated smoker walked back up to his ax and picked it up, intending to vent his anger by attacking the trees with a vengeance. After picking up his ax, he turned around and looked back down the mountain. Standing at the base of the trees, near where J B had left his rifle, was Man's buck. It just wasn't J B's day. Just then the buck turned and noticed the man looking at him.

"He must've had thirteen points on each side," said the old man, who still looked back with admiration.

"When he saw me, he lifted his head to lay his horns flat, and then he ran back into the woods. But even though he had his horns back as flat as he could get them, they still clicked against tree branches. It sounded just like it does when you draw a stick over the slats of a picket fence!"

The sight of the big buck almost left the mountain lad speechless. It was a case of "buck fever", even though there was no chance to shoot. J B was still almost dumbfounded when, shortly after, the hunters from up in the gap came by.

"Did you see Man's buck," they asked, but it was too late. The elusive buck, this phantom of the forest, was gone.

The hunters were from Mount Carmel, Northumberland County, and so the stories of Man's buck spread to that area as well. However, the big hart was only ever seen again one more time, when Jimmy Faust saw it one evening up in the same gap. After that, it seemed to disappear, leaving only its reputation and people wondering whether it was ever killed. [7]

Eventually even the biggest bucks fall to the persistent hunter, but even then there's no guarantee that the pursuer will get the trophy he's expecting. There can be difficulties, as one Lycoming County Nimrod found out about ten years ago.

Dave Poust, gifted taxidermist and avid hunter himself, is an eloquent raconteur of stories of the chase. His taxidermy shop, located along the waters of Pine Creek and near the village of Waterville, Lycoming County, sits on ground thought to be the site where pioneer hunter Philip Tome once had a cabin. The last vestiges of the cabin's foundation were washed away in the big flood of 1979. However, the mountains around the place are as beautiful and as rugged today as they were in Tome's era, and so they afford "miles to wander" for the deer and other wildlife that make these hills their home. This magnificent isolation allows many deer to avoid the hunter's bullets for years, and so some of the males grow beautiful sets of antlers. A visit to Poust's taxidermy shop during deer season will be rewarded with a view of the heads of one or more of these trophy bucks that were brought there for mounting. However, out of all the big racks he's seen over the decades, Poust still likes to recall the one that almost had to be thrown away. He's no doubt reminded of the tale every time he walks outside his shop and looks to the south and sees the lofty peak of Short Mountain in Clinton County.

One evening about ten years ago a friend of Poust's named Jim Stuchell shot a beautiful buck on top of Short Mountain. Stuchell dragged the buck down off the mountain top to a logging road, intending to drag it down to his vehicle from there. However, it was getting late, and it was still a mile or more to his car. The tired hunter decided to let the deer lie right where it was since he knew there were no hunters above him anymore that evening, and no vehicles on top of the mountain either. Convinced that there was nobody up there but himself, he started to walk down the ridge. Back at the Knights Hunting Camp, some of the hunters had noticed Stuchell's car was still there, and so they had decided to wait for him to come out of the woods before they started for home.

When Stuchell finally did emerge from the forest, he was relieved to see the men still at the camp. "Oh boy, I'm glad somebody's still here", he exclaimed. "I have a big buck up here I have to get!"

The dead deer was lying in a section of the mountain that could only be reached by a four wheel drive vehicle, and the only man left at camp with this kind of transportation was Thomas Roup, who was a Lycoming County judge at that time. Despite the fact that the vehicle was a "beat up" old Jeep, all the hunters left at the camp decided they'd help get the deer. The rest of the story is best told by Dave Poust.

"They started up the mountain, and by then it's pitch dark," recalled Dave in his entertaining style.

"They got to a real sharp horseshoe turn in the road, which was an eighth of a mile from where the deer lay, and got stuck in a mud hole in a rut. The road was in really bad shape, so everybody got out and decided they would push, and Tom would drive and try to get out of the mud hole.

"So he told them, 'If I get going, I'm going to keep on going so I can get out of this muddy area.'

"They said, 'If you get it movin' go right on up 'til you get to the deer'. 'I laid it right in the middle of the road. You can't miss it. It's right up here about an eighth of a mile.'

"They started pushing, and got the Jeep moving. So they hollered, 'Keep on going, we'll walk up!'

"When they got up there, the Jeep is in an odd angle, and both driver's side tires were off on the berm of the road, on the steep side. And the Jeep was just hanging there. It was ready to roll over, and when they got there they found out that both tires on that side were flat and the deer was underneath the vehicle! He ran over the deer and flattened both tires with the antlers!

"It was a big eleven point, and he had broken four or five of the points off. They had an awful time, but they managed to get the deer out from underneath the Jeep, picking up as many points as they could find. Then they couldn't drive that car, so they had to go back down to the camp, and by that time it's seven thirty, eight o'clock, and they only had a two wheel drive left.

"So they came down here to my shop. I was working on a deer, taxidermy, and they told me, 'We have a problem!'

"I looked at them, and they were wet, were all sweated, and their hair looked like they had been in a thunder shower. All I could think of was that someone was either dead or hurt. I asked if everyone was alright.

'Oh yes. That's not the problem! We have a deer up there we can't get down.'

"So they told me the whole story. A neighbor boy had a four wheeler, so we put a rope in from my Jeep and took the four wheeler up and brought the deer down here to my shop. We had to go up the next day with two different 'come alongs' and three jacks to get the car back on the road. We got it up, and I had two extra Jeep wheels here, so we got it patched up again so we could get his Jeep off the mountain.

"Roup actually ran over the deer. He never saw it because it was real steep and the headlights were actually shooting right over it, and it was lying on its belly and blended right in. They never knew what they hit until they had two flat tires! Fortunately, the next day when we went up to get the Jeep, we found the rest of the broken points. We repaired everything, and mounted the head for him. It came out perfect. You can't see a broken point anywhere!

"He's still being kidded about it. Every time somebody shoots a deer, they say, 'Tie Tom up so he can't run over my deer!' [8]

Poust doesn't agree with Cliff Vonada that there are fewer and fewer of these big bucks every year.

"I tell you what, " he contended. "The racks we got in this past season – I've been in business since '42 – we've never had a year when we've had so many big racks. Best year we ever had! The strongest survive, and when you have fewer deer, you have better feed. Therefore they develop better antlers.

"At Knights Hunting Club, when I started to hunt there, we had so many deer it wasn't even a sport; deer everywhere! You'd put on a drive, and see upwards of seventy-five to one-hundred deer come out in one drive. We would try to thin some of the does out, but we were still getting three, fives, and seven point bucks, and all our racks were small and twisted. Now we're getting nice bucks, but we only have about ten percent of the deer we once had." [8]

Footnote:

Dave's comments will be welcomed by those who think the best hunting days in the state are over. For anyone who still needs further proof that they are not, they should pay a visit to the Poust taxidermy shop in late December or in early January. It's at this time that Dave is his busiest, mounting the heads of the big trophy bucks that serve as reminders of the old days. However, these relics of the hunt also remind us that the mountains that the deer call home are still there, calling us to them when we wish to feel either as wild and free as the winds that whisper in the hemlocks or as tranquil as the murmur of an ever rolling stream.

Mackeyville Hunters, circa. 1920
Taken in front of Smull's Store
Mackeyville, Clinton County
(Cliff Vonada is fourth from left in front row)

Cliff Vonada with wife Vera, and the "Shovel" Buck
(Mackeyville, Clinton County)

GOD'S WARRIORS

What gives a man (and today I guess we'd have to say "or a woman" as well) the strength to go into war? Is it a sense of duty fired by patriotism, or is it a feeling that an injustice needs to be corrected? Fiery speeches and inflammatory writings are the catalysts that decide the issue for some men, but there are others who seem to have an inborn sense of duty that pulls them into the awful chaos of battle. There are many shining examples of unsung heroes like this, but anyone looking for one of them in Pennsylvania need search no further than Jacob Karstetter of Sugar Valley in Clinton County.

Born in 1806, "Jake" Karstetter was the son of one of the first settlers in the pretty little valley that was named for the abundance of sugar maple trees that once could be found here. Although he grew up with the sturdy descendants of other Sugar Valley pioneers, Jake was a "peculiar case". Blessed with exceptional physical strength and an ability to come out the winner in almost any fight in which he participated, and it was said Jake "was never willing to stand back", he was also a "splendid" shot.

The sharpshooter was so good with his trusty rifle, in fact, that when he took aim he was "dead sure for the 'bull's eye' " every time. Discouraged by his accuracy, Jake's opponents complained long and loudly enough that eventually he was not allowed to participate in the local shooting matches held throughout the region. However, when the Civil War broke out in '61, Jake was determined that his skill with rifle and ball would no longer be denied.

Exactly what inspired the Sugar Valley farmer to enlist in the Union army is not recorded, but whatever the motivation, he was "eager for the fray". However, Jake was fifty-four years old at the time and was told by an enlistment officer that he was too old to be "mustered in". Unable to change the army's mind, the determined patriot decided to try another approach, even if it meant stretching the truth a bit. So some time later Jake went to another enlistment office and here reported his age as forty-four. That was good enough for the recruiting officer there, and so Jake went off to war with the Seventh Pennsylvania, only to end up in the notorious Libby prison near Richmond, Virginia.

After spending an extended period in that Confederate "prison pen", the fifty-six year old Karstetter returned home and settled down to a peaceful life as a farmer. However, it wasn't long before he got the urge to "join the fray" once more. Realizing he would be refused because of age again, Jake contacted Andrew Gregg Curtin, Pennsylvania's famous "war governor", to plead his case. Curtin directed the feisty farmer to a surgeon who refused him anyway. However, Jake found out "on the sly" that if he paid two-hundred and sixty dollars he could be "put through".

Not to be denied, the "stout and rugged" patriot paid two hundred dollars to become a soldier, at a time when others were paying even more than that to stay out of the army.

Jacob Karstetter's war record was even more amazing than his fight to go to war in the first place. He fought in over twenty battles, serving part of that time as a sharpshooter. Officers found it hard to keep the independent marksman interested in company duty, and so sometimes allowed him to "go off now and then to have a few shots all to himself". However, one of John S. Mosby's Rebel sharpshooters returned the favor one night when Jake was on picket duty. The Confederate's shot was a near miss, cleanly taking off two of the Federal picket's fingers. [1]

Jake survived the war, spending the rest of his days back in Sugar Valley, but whether he mellowed or not in his old age is open to question. Sometimes old soldiers don't fade away quietly, and if Jake Karstetter was as cantankerous as another Civil War vet from the same valley, he would not have gone out without a fight

The older residents of Sugar Valley still remember some of the veterans of the Civil War – elderly men who were still alive when these residents, now elderly themselves, were young boys. A conversation with one of these folks provides a free ticket for a pleasurable journey into the past, and "trips" such as this are one of the fringe benefits of collecting the old-time tales: interesting anecdotes that reveal the human interest side of the olden times. You never know when such memories are going to surface, but on a pleasant summer afternoon while sitting on a front porch in Loganton, a Sugar Valley octogenarian recalled one such episode to several engrossed listeners. We followed intently as the story was told, accompanied now and then by the clatter of horses' hooves as Amish buggies passed by on the main street below.

"Henry Wren was a character," said the old farmer. 'Hen', we were told, was highly decorated for bravery in the Civil War, and, when he got older he wanted to get a government pension for his services. Grover Cleveland was president at the time the vet applied for his stipend, and Wren didn't anticipate any problems. He was one of the most decorated Civil War vets in Sugar Valley, and a pension for such a hero would surely be readily approved. However, due to some bureaucratic error or because of faulty records, his request was denied.

The denial infuriated the old soldier. In a fit of anger he wrote a letter to the president's wife, or at least that's what the oral history relates. If such an epistle was mailed and received, Mrs. Cleveland must have been surprised when she read it. The complaint itself would not have offended her, but the ending sentences contained language that would certainly have shocked her tender sensibilities, or those of any other member of the Victorian age's "fairer sex". Wren, it is said, ended his note with the statement that "she could kiss his ass if the old man [President Cleveland] didn't want to give him a pension". The valley folktales don't go on to state whether Henry Wren ever got his pension or not. [2]

How Henry Wren, Jake Karstetter, or anyone else, could so whole-heartedly throw themselves into the dangers of war is hard for most people to comprehend, and it's even harder for many to understand why any "man of the cloth" would voluntarily elect to participate in an activity once described by Union general William T. Sherman as "hell". However, throughout history religious leaders have struggled with ways to reconcile their religious beliefs and their convictions, with many concluding that they too needed to "join the fray", just like the old soldier from Sugar Valley.

Here in Pennsylvania there are several notable instances of clerics that seem to have made exceptional contributions as soldiers. Their stories can be found in the history books, and a few of these are worth mentioning. However, it will be seen that missing from all these historical examples is a minister of the Civil War era. It's hard to believe that no outstanding cleric-turned-soldier surfaced during that period of exceptional sacrifice, but if there was such a man, historical records seem to have passed him by. Local legend, on the other hand, indicates otherwise, and it's this man's story that should finally be told.

Anyone who remembers their Pennsylvania history or who has read the previous volumes in the *Pennsylvania Fireside Tales* series will recall the many terrible episodes of warfare that echoed and rumbled over Pennsylvania's hills during its first two hundred years of white occupation. From the time it was founded in 1681 until the Civil War dyed its soil with blood in the 1860's, Pennsylvania saw its share of conflict.

No one living on Pennsylvania's frontier during the first half of the eighteenth century could have anticipated the terrible and tragic episodes that would occur during the French and Indian Wars of the 1750's. Perhaps that's why, when the war clouds came, every able-bodied frontiersman, including some "sky pilots", as ministers were called in a much later age, became soldiers. Events were too threatening, too horrible, for anyone except the most ardent pacifist to consider other options, including Presbyterian minister John Steel.

Steel's first church was located along the west branch of the Conococheague Creek, probably somewhere in present-day Franklin County, about 1755. At that time the chapel was surrounded by a stockade, due to the many Indian incursions into the region, and Reverend Steel organized a company of riflemen to serve as a defensive unit. Most of the Scotch-Irishmen in the regiment were Steel's parishioners. They not only respected him as the leader of their church, but also were as determined as he was to defend the homes and farms they had bought with their sweat and tears, and so it seemed natural to elect him as their Captain. Despite the dangers of the times, Reverend Steel faithfully conducted church services every Sunday, but as a matter of prudent caution the minister and most of the men in the congregation always had their trusty flintlocks and ammunition by their sides. And so it was that Reverend Steel's little church in the wildwood became known to history as Fort Steel.

Several years later the Reverend Steel was even more active in the protection of the frontier, being placed in charge of Fort Allison, near Carlisle. Here, it is said, the parishioners also carried their muskets to church, and minister Steel would bring his, hanging it and his hat on a wall peg behind the pulpit. One Sunday in the middle of a service, a messenger rushed in with the news that the Indians had just murdered the Walker family near Rankin's Mill. Services were quickly ended, and with the parson leading the way, the men in the congregation "went in pursuit of the murderers." [3]

The end of the French and Indian wars of the 1750's brought only momentary peace to the Pennsylvania hills. Ten years later the Indians of the Ohio and Allegheny valleys, led by the great Ottawa chieftain Pontiac, made a determined attempt to sweep white invaders from their lands. Once more the pioneers of Pennsylvania heard the war whoop and the scalp halloo, and defense was again the watchword of the times.

Among the determined white defenders of the pioneer settlements during the stirring years of "Pontiac's War" was Presbyterian minister John Elder of Paxtang, present-day Dauphin County. Here, in the shadows of the Blue Mountains, the Scotch-Irish settlers had no faith that the peace-loving Quakers in Philadelphia would provide money or troops for the defense of what in those days was the western frontier. Provisions for dealing with Indian marauders would have to be made by the frontiersmen themselves, and so every man once again became a soldier, including Reverend Elder.

Apparently being a man of action, John Elder recruited men from his congregation and formed a company of mounted rangers whose mission was to protect the Paxton settlements from Indian raiders. Although they should be given credit for the lives they saved, the "Paxton Boys" are best remembered for their slaughter of innocent Conestoga Indians at the Lancaster County jail in 1763. It was a black mark which will eternally besmirch the names of the Paxtang rangers, but John Elder's is not included in that infamous list. Elder tried to convince his men not to go; they couldn't, he insisted, tell the guilty from the innocent, but when the men threatened to shoot his favorite horse, the "fighting parson of Paxtang", as he became known, had to step aside. [4] Later he might have had second thoughts about his involvement in matters of warfare when he heard about the Indian children, squaws, and old men the rangers indiscriminately massacred that day,

It would appear that Presbyterians had a monopoly on fighting parsons during the 1750's and 1760's in Pennsylvania, but in the decade after Pontiac's War there was a Lancaster County Presbyterian cleric who had a different outlook than John Elder or John Steel.

Preserved in the annals of the Donegal Presbyterian Church in Lancaster County is the story of the "Witness Tree", which stood in front of the sanctuary until about twenty years ago when blight and old age finally claimed it. It was around this giant oak, so says the old legend which clings to the ancient church to this day, that the entire congregation formed a circle in June of 1777, and while holding hands, pledged their fidelity to the Revolution and to the Colonial government. Their minister, however, was not amused, steadfastly proclaiming that his sympathies rested with King George rather than with the colonists.

The minister's political opinions were tolerated, but not accepted. Finally one Sunday morning, sometime after the congregation's declaration of support for the Revolution, the Tory pastor was in the middle of the church service when he was interrupted by a horseman who had traveled at break-neck speed to announce that General Washington needed men to help defend Philadelphia from the British, Reverend McFarquhar, still maintaining his allegiance to the king, spoke out against the request, whereupon his congregation dragged the helpless cleric out to the witness tree and made him "raise his hat in allegiance to the Revolution." [5]

The memory of the Donegal church's Tory minister has almost been swept into the dust bins of history over the years, and that seems a proper fate when the story of another minister of that same period is recalled.

John Peter Gabriel Muhlenberg was not a typical Pennsylvania "Dutchman". Born in 1746 to German immigrants in Eastern Pennsylvania, Muhlenberg was a natural born leader of men. However, this grandson of the great Indian agent Conrad Weiser chose to heed the call of the church, and so became a Luthern minister. His first parish was in the Shenandoah Valley of Virginia where his leadership qualities were recognized by Colonial authorities. Then, in 1776, the young minister was asked by these same authorities to raise a regiment of soldiers who would become part of Washington's army. Muhlenberg kept his assignment a secret until the next Sunday's church service when he wore a full Continental officer's uniform underneath his ministerial robes.

Using Ecclesiastes III as his text, the thirty-year-old cleric inspired his congregation with a rousing sermon, concluding with the famous lines: "For everything its season, and for every activity under heaven its time: a time to be born and a time to die; ... a time for war and a time for peace." Then, pausing for effect, the young officer pulled open his robe, revealing his officer's uniform, and thundered, "There is a time to pray and a time to fight; now is the time to fight!"

History records that hundreds of stalwart men joined Muhlenberg's regiment, and also notes that the cleric-turned-soldier was so effective in his military role that he ended that career as a major general. He also came out of the war with a nickname that revealed the respect enemy soldiers had for their crafty adversary. Impressed by his military prowess, the king's Hessian troops called the general *Teufel Piet.* It meant "Devil Pete". [6]

Twenty more years passed after the end of the Revolutionary War before war clouds once again darkened the war-torn hills of the Keystone State. The War of 1812, like its predecessors, produced heroes worthy of mention in any histories of the times, and among those heroes was Reverend William Johnston of Dunlaps Creek in Fayette County.

Convinced that the people of Uniontown and surrounding communities were not behind the war as much as they should be, the fiery cleric marched into the Uniontown courthouse one day in 1814 and preached a hellfire-and-damnation sermon about reasons the war effort should be supported. Using Jeremiah 48, verse 10, as his text ("Cursed be he that keepeth back his sword from blood"), Johnston inspired one-hundred and eighteen men to enlist on the spot. However, the young minister had also managed to fire up the anti-war groups in the town, who thereafter called him the "Bloody Parson". It was a name that stuck with him until the day he died. [7]

After the War of 1812, the gods of strife were satisfied for almost fifty more years until they needed to see blood spilled upon Pennsylvania's soil once again. This time it was the Civil War that they would send down upon the state's peaceful hills and valleys, and in some respects it was the worst war of all in terms of the human toll it exacted. Men from all walks of life were drawn into and destroyed by the great conflict, including ministers of many different denominations. However, none of these clerics seem to stand out in history like a Captain John Steel, and none of them have left their marks on the historical record like the "Fighting Parson of Paxtang", *Teufel Piet* Muhlenberg, or the "Bloody Parson" of Uniontown. In fact, it would seem that the clergy of that era was less apt to pick up the sword than any of their predecessors, but legends and folktales, at least in one case, paint a different picture in that regard.

The story of Lewis Edmonds, minister of a Reformed church in the small Centre County town of Aaronsburg during the Civil War, has been forgotten by the present generation. It was never a tale that was widely heard, and even thirty years ago there were few residents of the area who could still remember it. In fact, one of the last men, if not the very last one, who could recall the episode died in the 1980's. He had heard about it when he was just a boy, and so even though the exact details were sketchy, the salient points were well-remembered and form an intriguing addition to the legendary annals of the Civil War.

Not everyone north of the Mason-Dixon line was a supporter of Mr. Lincoln's war. Some of these more determined secessionists, known as "copperheads" or "seceshs" by northern sympathizers, formed secret organizations to undermine the federal war effort in any way they could, including using intimidation if they thought it would work. It is remembered by some that an organization called the Knights of the Golden Circle used such tactics, and their "coffin notices" added yet another bitter ingredient to the bubbling cauldron that had boiled over and drenched the land with the terrible stench of war.

Whenever the Knights in Columbia County found out that a young man there was thinking of enlisting as an officer in the Union army, they would attempt to discourage him by sending him an empty coffin with a malicious message inside. The same organization was also active south of Nittany Mountain in John Penn's Valley of Centre County.

There were many young Penns Valley men who marched off to war and gave the folks at home reasons to be proud, but the area also had nests of Copperheads who helped other recruits avoid service altogether. In the mountains south of Penns View, near the little village of Coburn, it is said that there was a "deserters' camp" where a draftee would be sent to "lay low" until the authorities gave up looking for him. At one time there were as many as thirty-four deserters in the camp, and "a large group of citizens would provide them with clothes, food, and ammunition." [8]

Anti-war sentiment ran high at times in other valley communities too, culminating in one case with an effigy burning by war protestors. In Haines Township there were anti-war sentiments as well, with one draft evader shooting himself in the toe to avoid service, and another hiding in a cave until the end of the war. These were individual acts, but many of Aaronsburg's citizens were in sympathy, especially those who were members of Lewis Edmonds' congregation.

Edmonds' opinions on the war were no secret. He was a supporter of the conflict with the south, but he was in a position much like that of the notorious McFarquhar of Donegal Church during the Revolution. Members of Edmonds' church were anti-war men, and they had made it clear to him that if he enlisted they would fire him. Undaunted, and perhaps familiar with the story of how Peter Muhlenberg surprised his congregation by wearing a uniform under his clerical robes, Edmonds, according to local legend, did the same thing. Wearing the blue uniform of a Union soldier under his black gown, the brave young minister walked into the church and conducted the service as usual. Then in the middle of his sermon, he pulled open his robe and announced he was "going off to war". [9]

Valley folktales say that Lewis Edmonds survived the war and came back to live in a house in High Valley, above Coburn. Here, below the lofty peaks of the White Mountains, Edmonds spent his final years, passing away peacefully and gradually fading out of peoples' memories. A family of mountain folks moved into the vacant house shortly after the old soldier's death, but eventually they began to tell their neighbors that they couldn't sleep at night.

Unnatural sounds kept them awake, they said. The loudest noises reminded them of chains rattling, but that cacophony would always die down. It was the following, less strident sound, one that was almost as soft as a whisper, that proved to be the most unnerving to the isolated mountaineers.

They all knew the story of Lewis Edmonds and how he hid his army uniform under his ministerial robe, and the softer noise they heard at night sounded to them just like a heavy garment being dragged over the floors of the house. Unable to stand the nocturnal doings any longer, the "hill hawks" decided to leave, and they probably moved out on an April Fool's day, the typical day for "flittings" in the Pennsylvania Dutch regions. [10]

The Edmonds' place was occupied by a series of other families over the years, but whether it was just too isolated, or whether it was too haunted, eventually no one wanted to live there, and the old place gradually fell into disrepair. However it did not lose its appeal to humans entirely.

As the deserted homestead became more and more haunted looking, people began to recall the stories of the noises that drove residents away, and local teenagers were attracted to the house, seeing it as a place where they could test their mettle by spending a night inside. But as nothing out of the ordinary was ever heard by any of them, they, too, left the place to its ghosts. It was the final nail in Lewis Edmonds' coffin. His story and his name were forgotten by all but a few of those teenagers, one of whom told the story to me in 1972 when he was an old man.

Footnotes:

Records from the German Reformed Church in Aaronsburg list the ministers who served that charge, starting in 1852. Included in that roll is the name L. C. Edmunds.

In the muster roll of the 148th Pennsylvania Volunteers for August 28, 1862, is the name of second lieutenant Lewis C. Edmonds of Haines Township, Centre County.[11] Edmonds couldn't have joined a better squad. General James Beaver's regiment was a well-trained and well-disciplined fighting unit, qualities that would serve them well during later engagements at places like Cold Harbor, Hatcher's Run, and Chancellorsville. However, one other quality distinguished "Jimmy" Beaver's outfit, and that was the General's habit of leading his men in prayer everyday. It was a practice that must have delighted Lewis Edmonds, and it also certainly impressed other Federal troops, who referred to the 148th as "the praying regiment". [12]

An account of the day Lewis Edmonds wore his uniform to church is preserved in Muffley's *History of the 148th Pennsylvania Volunteers* (see page 618). However, this account makes no mention of Edmonds concealing his uniform under his clerical gown. Apparently the stories of Peter Muhlenberg and that of Lewis Edmonds became intertwined over the years, making Edmonds that much more of a folk hero.

Reverend Lewis C. Edmonds

148th Pennsylvania Volunteers

(Picture from Muffley's *History of the 148th*)

MAN'S BEST FRIEND(LY GHOST)

In all my years of collecting folktales I've met quite a few fascinating storytellers, but I've never found many "Pennsylvania Dutchmen" as unique as L. W. Bumbaugh. Known locally as "Mountain Bummy", the former hobo-turned-herbalist and seller of rare books knew many interesting tales of the Blue Mountains, and his heavy Pennsylvania Dutch accent made the accounts even more entertaining. His quaint store was located in the small Berks County community of Niantic, and he was probably considered the town "character" by his tradition-steeped neighbors. Whenever I visited "Bummy" I always came away with another legend for my collection, but I also left with the feeling that it was the shop's interior that colored the tales and made them more appealing than they would have been had they been recited in some modern-day setting.

The old place was badly in need of paint, and the floors sagged, squeaking in protest whenever someone walked over a particularly loose board. The windows always needed washed, and the shelves inside looked as though they hadn't been dusted in months. Antiquated medicine jars filled with dried herbs and labeled with old-style apothecary decals sat on some of the shelves along the walls of the place, and row upon row of book cases stacked with musty smelling old books took up most of the floor space. Hanging from the ceiling were clusters of dried herbs, just like those that original pioneer families once used for medicinal purposes, and they combined with the other surroundings to set the mood for a story of the long ago. Bunches of drying bergamont, golden seal, yarrow, and tansy emitted strange odors unfamiliar to us, and somehow the smells always seemed to attune our senses to that frequency which is most responsive to tales of an untouchable and bygone age.

On one particular visit, late in August, we walked into the old man's store and found things had not changed much since the last time we were there. After spending some pleasant time looking over his inventory of books, we walked into a back room where we found the herbalist, brewing himself a cup of tansy tea. He was in a talkative mood, perhaps soothed by his warm brew, and on this day he was reminded of a story his grandmother used to tell him, and which, he thought, would be of interest to us.

"My grandmother had a fantastic name," he began.

"You can't believe this! Her name was Cevilla Andorra Elizabeth Weller. Her real father was killed in the Civil War, and then her mother remarried a man name Treichler. When she got married she married a Lea; she was tired of long names, so she got a short one, L-E-A. But she used all three. So this was her handle: Cevilla Andorra Elizabeth Weller Treichler Lea.

"When she was a young girl, she worked. You know they hired young people out them days, way back in the 1860's and

1870's, and she was working for these people up around Breinigsville (Lehigh County). She was thirteen or fourteen, and worked as a maid over in there in the Furnace Hills. Somewhere she had to go through the woods to get to the place and to come back from work. She never said where she was staying. She was probably staying with somebody around the Huff's Church area because I know she used to take me up there to visit a lot of the people.

"And she swears that when she was going through the woods - and this happened not just one time, but a lot of times. She said this happened on and off a lot of times when she went through the woods. This big black dog came alongside of her. It had great big eyes, she said. 'Eyes as big as saucers', is the way she would often say in later years. "She could talk to it, and she could reach down and she could feel it, but the body wasn't there! She'd see it, and then she wouldn't see it!

"But this used to walk alongside of her. She claimed it was protecting her through the woods. Some ghost from someplace, you know, that came in the form of this dog to protect her while she was going through the woods, because when she come out of the woods, boom! It was gone. It was just through the woods."

I then asked the old-timer whether the young maid's parents ,or anyone else, believed her enough to try to see the sable apparition themselves. The appearance of a ghostly dog, or a live wolf, would have piqued the curiosity of more than one person, and since solitary wolves were still found in some of the wilder parts of Pennsylvania as late as the 1880's, anything that sounded like it might be one of these lone survivors would surely have gotten the attention of local hunters. However, if there was more of the story to tell, the young mountain maid, this Little Red Riding Hood of the Blue Mountains, never mentioned it. It was up to her descendants to decide for themselves just what the young girl might have seen.

"She always told the same story when talking about this experience with the ghost dog," recalled the herbalist. "Now I knew my grandmother as a truthful woman, a very religious woman, and she swore by this," he averred "She said, 'this is positively true! That's what happened." [1]

We'll never know, of course, exactly what it was that the young servant girl saw on those dark nights when she most needed a friend to guide her through the forbidding forest. However, it appears that the account is a story that, at one time, was equivalent to what today we'd call an "urban legend". This same episode, with some variations, was collected in Carbon County in the first decades of the last century; and still another variant was circulated in the mid-1940's in Lancaster County.

The Carbon County version also has a "young servant girl" as its heroine. This mountain maid worked close enough to her parents that she could return home every night, similar to the girl in the last tale. Since she had to pass by a deserted stretch of woodland on the way, she always tried to get back before nightfall. One evening she was late, and darkness fell before she got to the woods. At that point she noticed a man walking beside her. He did not reply when she bid him a "Good Evening", but she was still glad to have some company when she walked by the frightening forest. However, when she warned her silent companion, "who was wearing a good suit of dark clothes", about a mud puddle on the road ahead, there was a loud noise from the woods, as though trees were falling and branches breaking, and "fiery balls shot up from the ground". Without a moment's hesitation, the young lady, it is stated, "ran on home as fast as her legs could carry her". [2]

Back in the 1940's a Lancaster County lad was badly frightened by a nocturnal apparition as well, one that did not have a human appearance. In this case the youth might have been comforted had he been able to compare notes with miss Cevilla of Berks County.

One frosty moonlit evening in October of 1944, the young man was pedaling his bike past the Lloyd Mifflin estate in West Hempfield Township of Lancaster County. One of the fifteen-year-old's regular chores was to go for coal-oil, and on this night he was on the return leg of his journey. The ancient Mifflin place, with its long front porch, high windows, and tall dark pine trees in the front yard, always looks a little bleak, especially at night when it's bathed in pale moonlight and the night wind is soughing in the somber pines. People passing by the old estate are often struck by its decidedly haunted look, but the effect is even more pronounced in the month of October when thoughts of Halloween are on the mind.

No one would probably be more surprised about the effect that his "Norwood" has on people than Lloyd Mifflin, who resided there during the 1880's. Mifflin no doubt would expect that the legacy of warmth and beauty he left behind still surrounds his estate with the same aura. His paintings and poetry made him famous, and no one could argue that his poem "In the Fields" would not be enough to light up anyone's day:

When daily greener grows the oats;
When near his nest the red-wing floats,
And sweetbrier blossoms in the lane;
When freshening wind the wheat-field shakes,
And in its billowing rolling makes
An ocean of the grain: [3]

However, on this particular night in 1944, as the young man on the bicycle pedaled down the road approaching the Mifflin place, he noticed a big black dog coming out of the woods opposite Norwood. The boy stopped to pet the apparently friendly canine, but when he reached down to touch its head, his hand passed right through it, "touching nothing but thin air"! As though bored with the whole encounter, the dog then turned away and passed through the front wheel of the bike, just as though there were no spokes there at all. In a state of panic, the cyclist reached his aunt's house, which was just down the road, in record time. She would later say that she had never "seen anyone so frightened" as her nephew on that haunted October night. His parents weren't as sympathetic, probably thinking that their son was looking for an excuse to avoid some work, and they still required the young man to make his daily trip for coal-oil. However, it is said that from then on he always made his trips before sundown. [4]

I've come across many versions of this story, and each one seems to have its own little twist. One thing that's safe to say, however, is that the dog does travel a lot.

Over in Schuylkill County, near the village of Cressona sometime during the first decades of the twentieth century, a big black dog "appeared from nowhere" between two boys who were walking along Seven Stars Road. When one of the boys, a dog lover at heart, went to pet it, "just like the snap of a finger, it disappeared"! The shot of adrenaline that went through his body at that point allowed the frightened young man to run the two miles to his home "in record time". [5]

Up in Clearfield County, on the mountains near Penfield, there is an unsettled and remote area where some say yet another ghost dog has frightened travelers in the night. Perhaps it's this dog that led people to name the area what they did, or perhaps it was the unexplainable forces that ruined a lumbering operation's equipment here in the 1920's, but in any case the area today is called Spook Hollow. The account of the vandalized lumber trucks and bulldozers is another entire story, and it will be included in one of my future volumes, but the tale of the ghost dog of Spook Hollow deserves some mention here, if for no other reason than to give the reader an idea as to the type of legends that sometimes cling to places with "haunted" names.

The Boy Scouts own most of the Spook Hollow wilderness today, but sometime in the distant past a mining operation was established by the crossroads near the present site of the Boy Scout Camp. During the heydays of the mining camp, a grocery store and, say some locals, perhaps even a hotel, grew up around that same crossroads. It was near here, so says the legend, that a woman was murdered. Authorities apprehended a local ne'er-do-well, tried him, and found him guilty.

"He said he didn't do this," recalled a man who has hiked into Spook Hollow and also into the eerie hidden valley that's nearby. "He said that after he was hung, his dog would never let him leave the area; would protect him".

Ignoring what seemed to be the ravings of a madman on death row, the authorities hanged the accused man anyway, and then, and legend doesn't say why they chose this site, they buried him on the mountain that night.

"The next day they came back, and there was a big black dog sitting next to the gravesite," continued our storyteller.

"It had dug up the body, so they reburied it. Another time the dog ran off and dug up the body again, so they buried him deeper and put rocks over the gravesite. They came back the next morning, and the dog had evidently dug up the body again!"

"So what they did the third time, they chased the dog off and took the man's body and moved it to another area outside of the county.

"So now the dog, it would be a ghost by now, returns to that site, and keeps looking for this man's body in the Spook Hollow area. His ghost is supposed to come back and look for the body. The story is now that every so often people come by at night and hear the dog howling." [6]

I would have been surprised if, during all the years of my collecting, I had not found a story about a disembodied dog in the Seven Mountains country of Centre County. This section of the state seems to be one of the last repositories of the old mountain tales in Pennsylvania, and it was my feeling that a long-lived legend like the one of the disappearing ghost dog should have found a home somewhere in these old hills. Eventually I did find a life-long mountain man who said he could tell me a story like this. It had happened, he said, to a friend of his, who told him that such a dog could once be found down in the wilds of Decker Valley, in a secluded little cut in the mountains called Pole Bridge Hollow.

Named for a bridge made only of long wooden poles that spanned a narrow stream on Kohler Mountain, the hollow, it was once believed, was also home to a big black dog with no head. The spook dog, it is said, would appear on the pole bridge every night at midnight, just standing there silently, until someone approached the bridge.

"Old Claytie Auman, I don't know if you ever talked to him, told me that story himself," began the mountaineer who loved to tell the tales he had heard from the old-timers.

"The road past the [mountain] cemetery goes back to the Crater place. There used to be a farm back there. He said him and his wife were going back to the Crater place to schnitz apples or to make apple butter. They were walking with a lantern, and when they left there to come back, that dog was standing on top of that old bridge. He said him and his wife seen it. He said it was a black dog, and it had no head! They went up towards the bridge, and he said it just disappeared!"

"He said, 'That dog had no head! I saw that with my own eyes!' "

"Clayt swore to that. He said, 'That I saw!' [7]

Tales of encounters like this can be attributed to the overactive imaginations of nervous gentlemen, or to the fertile imaginations of gifted storytellers. However, episodes about specter hounds are not new to the timeless world of legends. Accounts of "black headless dog-fiends" could be heard in northern England, around Lancashire, in 1825, and in all probability were widely disseminated throughout Europe for centuries. [8]

Scholars say the notion of the specter hound dates back to medieval times when stories of the Norse god Odin and his "furious host" of baying hounds still struck a chord of terror in the hearts of the masses. Other folklorists theorize that the large "saucer" eyes the ghost dogs are sometimes described as having "are suggestive of connections with natural phenomena like lightning or *ignis-fatuus* (Will-o'-the-wisp)". [8] It would seem, however, that the basic source of such stories can be traced to mans' deep-rooted fears of the supernatural and unknown. In Pennsylvania Dutchland, for example, legends which can often be traced to tales that had their origins in ancient Europe tell of individuals selling their souls to the devil. People passing by the homes of the sell-outs at night would, it was claimed, sometimes "meet a large black dog with blazing eyes – the devil come to plan evil with his servant". [9]

Such ideas would be enough to cause anyone's imagination to run wild if they found themselves passing through a thick woods by themselves one night and suddenly saw something that at first looks like a dog, but which may be nothing more than a trick of moonlight and shadow. However, fear of the dark, and the evil waiting to pounce on us it might be concealing, seems to be one of mankind's natural instincts, and so the mind convinces the person that the shadows are really a specter hound. However, people who have seen such things are often described as "truthful" and "religious", and they believe they haven't been deceived by some dancing shadows. So, for whatever the reason, stories of encounters with ghostly dogs persist, ranging from tales of harmless meetings to episodes that reflect our instinctive fear of the dark and the evil we think it hides.

RAVENS' KNOB

Stagecoach travel in the 1800's seems to us today, when viewed through the rose-colored lens of nostalgia, to have been a pleasant and stress-free form of transportation. In reality, however, a long trip by "coach-and-four" was often not a pleasant experience, and could, in fact, be "exhausting". [1]

Stage routes in the early 1800's were usually nothing more than a "succession of mud-holes with an occasional corduroy" [1], and the resultant ride was what might be expected. In the words of one delicate English lady who traveled through part of Pennsylvania by stagecoach in 1830, passengers were "tossed about like a few potatoes in a wheelbarrow."[1] So much time was spent protecting "knees, elbows and heads", she complained, that passengers did not have "leisure to look out of the windows"! [1]

If the women who traveled by stage had such strong complaints, then it would seem as though "insult was added to injury" in the case of the male passengers. Men "usually walked up the hills," [2] wrote one historian, recalling the stage coach days of his youth, and at other times passengers might "be obliged to get out", recalled another early traveler, to "help the coachman lift the coach out of a quagmire or rut." [1]

Sometimes heavy rains did change a stage road into a bog, extending what was normally a one day journey into two days or more. These kinds of weather-related problems, coupled with bitterly cold weather in the winter, presence of wild animals like mountain lions and wolves in the forests through which the stage routes ran, and the possibility that highwaymen might lie waiting in the wildest parts of the mountains, were among the risks a person would have to weigh if they were considering a trip by stage in the early 1800's. There were, however, some stops along the way that could afford a pleasant interlude, depending on the quality of the establishment.

Layovers at the various taverns and hotels along the stage routes were periodically made so fresh teams of horses could be harnessed to the coaches, and here passengers and drivers alike could buy food and drink, and give their jostled bodies some relief. Among the rest stops in central Pennsylvania were a few that were widely heralded for their particularly excellent food, warm accommodations, or good fellowship. In Centre County this elite group included Henry Roush's tavern in the Woodward Narrows near the Union County line, Ben Lucas' Rattlesnake Hotel on top of Rattlesnake Mountain near Unionville, and General John Potter's brick hotel in Potters Mills.

Although the first two establishments are no longer standing, Potter's place has withstood the tests of time, and can still be seen today. Most people who are familiar with the area remember the old hotel as the site of a fine dining establishment called the Eutaw House. Several restaurants of that name have tried to "make a go of it" here in the last several years, and rumor has it that another restaurant will open in the old place again soon. For now, however, (January, 2000), the ancient hostelry sits empty, frequented only by its ghosts, who, if they were asked, might recount some fascinating stories of the old coaching days.

There are probably many interesting accounts about passengers who "laid over" at the brick hotel when it was a regular stop along the stage line that ran between Lewistown, Mifflin County, and Bellefonte, Centre County. However, as years passed, and a new order of things replaced the old, memories of stage coaches, the passengers they carried, and the thrilling experiences they might have had, slowly faded away until almost all recollections of those days were forgotten. Now it's mainly just the history books that contain passages about that forgotten time, and those references are few and far between.

Old newspaper accounts have also preserved tidbits about the coaching days in this region, and it is in these articles that even lists of a few of the stage drivers can be found.. Names of men like Bill Horner, Nick Runkle, and Jim Weeds mean nothing to us today, but they were all familiar names to passengers who regularly road the stagecoaches over the Lewistown-Bellefonte Pike. [3] Although only their names remain behind, a pen picture of what these hardy characters looked like may be gleaned from a description of the coachmen that Charles

Dickens observed when he rode the stage from York to Harrisburg in 1842.

The drivers were, penned Dickens, "usually as dirty as the coach", with one "dressed like a very shabby English baker; the second like a Russian peasant." [4] Coachmen on the Bellefonte and Lewistown route may have looked the same as their southern counterparts, but today lovers of the past wonder more about what tales these men might have been able to share concerning the times when they sat atop their stages and guided four-horse teams along the narrow mountain highways, the crack of their bullskin whips echoing like pistol shots throughout the Seven Mountains.

If someone had talked to the old stage drivers when they were still alive, they might have been able to at least save some of the more interesting human interest stories that once clung to the popular stagecoach stop in Potters Mills. No one seems to have had the interest or time to interview the old fellows, but despite the apparent oversight there are a few tales about the place that have displayed an unusual reluctance to be forgotten, and there is one in particular that still causes people to pause, and wonder.

Among the most "notorious" individuals associated with the stagecoach stop on the Bellefonte-Lewistown Pike was the inn-keeper who ran the establishment for the Potters during the twelve year period from 1824 until 1838. John C. Coverly was a capable boniface, but he also cultivated a reputation as a "character". Although he was noted for setting "an excellent table", he was also famous for his story-telling ability, especially tales of the "tall" variety.

The genial host could apparently tell his stories in a most appealing and convincing way, making even the tallest ones sound true. One of his most famous stretches involved some Philadelphia gentlemen who had spent a night at the inn. Early the next morning when they came down for breakfast, Coverly started regaling them with his tales, including one about a very unusual local affair that occurred every morning at Taylor's Tavern in Pleasant Gap. Coverly described the event in such glowing terms that the city men decided to make a hard ride all the way over Nittany Mountain to Taylor's so they could get there before noon. Their affable host had them convinced that if they got there after twelve o'clock they would miss the daily migration of rattlesnakes that came down off the mountain to drink at Taylor's spring.

The Philadelphians, with coat tails flying, must have made quite a sight as their galloping horses followed the stage route through the tiny settlement of Centre Hill, past the quaint little hamlet of Earlystown, up over Nittany Mountain at the sleepy village of Black Hawk, and into Pleasant Gap. They arrived at Taylor's with high expectations, but when they told Taylor why they had come and who had sent them, the tavern-owner immediately decided to join in on the joke. Rather then telling the men that they had been sent on a "wild goose chase", Taylor solemnly declared that the snakes had already been down to the spring and had just gone back up the mountain. [5]

No doubt John Coverly had fun for years telling people about the Philadelphia "city slickers" he had sent over the mountain to watch some snakes that were never there. It's also probably safe to say that such noteworthy successes inspired him to seek even loftier heights. If so, then one notable example would have to be the tale that he sometimes told guests at the inn, even in the presence of his boss. Coverly, it was remembered, would unabashedly state that he owned the inn and the town's mills, and that the Potters were merely his tenants. General John Potter complained to Coverly one day about this bold-faced lie, but Coverly was unperturbed, replying, "You are very uncharitable, Mr. Potter, in not allowing a man to be happy a little while!" [5]

Coverly's reputation as a teller of tall tales was one which apparently stayed with him for the rest of his life. Another Philadelphian who often stayed at the Potters Mills hotel while checking on real estate interests in Centre County never forgot Coverly, even after the landlord left the Potters' employ and opened Coverly House in Harrisburg.

Mr. Diehl, many years afterward, had occasion to spend a night in the Coverly House, and while there struck up a conversation with Coverly's son Wells. Not knowing to whom he was speaking, Diehl recalled that he once knew a man named Coverly that kept one of the best hotels in Centre County. Wells, having his father's sense of humor, said he had been told about the same man, but that he was supposed to be "of no account".

Diehl was insistent, stating once again that the Centre County Coverly was an excellent innkeeper.

"Yes," Wells replied, "that might be, but he was not thought much of."

Diehl considered this for awhile, and then finally remarked, "When I come to think of it, he was the infernalist liar I ever heard talk!" [5]

After John Coverly left the Potters to start his own business in 1838, his former employers hired a man named Jacob Lebo to run their hotel at what was then called Potter's Bank. No human interest episodes from the days when Jacob Lebo was the Potters' innkeeper were apparently noteworthy enough to be passed on down to future generations, but there is one legendary account that has survived from that time, and it overshadows even the stories about John Coverly.

Sometime in 1839, during "Jake" Lebo's first year at the Potters' hotel, another Philadelphian got off the stage from Lewistown and requested a room at the inn. At least that's what the legend claims. He was a serious-looking, yet handsome man, about thirty years old, with mirthless eyes and thinning hair. Although no one may have given him a second glance, anyone noticing his melancholy countenance probably attributed it to the business that brought him here once they found out what that was. He had come to settle the estate of a recently-departed relative, so say the old accounts, and the business would take him back into the mountains nearby.

Though not nearly as eminent in 1839 as he would become after he, himself, had died ten years later, the irascible gentleman did have a number of published poems and stories to his credit; literary efforts that were characteristic of the many similar creations for which he was to become famous. Although the old inn at Potters Bank would have been a quiet setting for literary pursuits, the man's business was of a decidedly more practical nature, and these interests required him to journey back into the wildest parts of the somber mountains that stretched to the east.

It was on a trip into these same mountains one day, proclaims the legend, that the young adventurer met a pretty young mountain maid. Her name, according to the same legend, was Helena Hallferty Park.[6] It was "love at first sight" for the easily-enamored Philadelphian, but the local beauty was not as easily smitten. Although it must have been flattering to have a complete stranger fall so completely for her, Helena felt he was not her type. It was a rejection that was almost too much for the sensitive suitor to bear, and he tried to seek solace by wandering through the mountains, perhaps hoping to find another woman who was just as attractive as the first, yet more attuned to his soul.

During one of his solitary trips into the woods, the jilted paramour came to a panoramic overlook of range upon range of mountains. At the base of the steep banks of the overlook were miles and miles of dense forest which concealed deep hollows and a hidden valley that locals had named High Valley. What intrigued the depressed youth the most, however, or so the legend states, was the large number of birds that seemed to call the cliffs their home.

The fluttering avians looked like crows since they were coal black, but they were the much larger cousins of those birds, and they did like it here. The place was apparently their nesting ground, for the spot had been named "Ravens' Knob" after them. In fact, it was the mournful cries of the ravens and, on cloudier days, the weird charm of the spot, that supposedly drew the disenchanted Philadelphian back to it time and time again. It would have been a place that was lonely and bleak enough to fit his own temperament at the time, and it would have no doubt inspired him, if the story is true. For it was here, claim the local tellers of this tale, that the despondent young poet was inspired to write one of his most famous compositions. At this spot, they claim, Edgar Allan Poe penned in entirety his poem entitled "The Raven". [7]

There are those who would claim that the story of Edgar Allan Poe's visit to Potters Mills in Centre County sounds more like a tale that came straight from the mouth of the "Infernalist liar" of that same town. Given John Coverly's talent for telling such stories, it would not be surprising if the Poe tale were one of these; and if he did concoct the legend, then Coverly's spirit would probably still be laughing today, wherever it might be, because scholars and laymen alike have wondered for decades whether the story of Poe's visit has any basis in fact or not.

Scholars who have studied Edgar Allan Poe and his works would say that the poet never made it as far west as Centre County in his Pennsylvania travels, and even if he did find his way to Ravens' Knob in the Seven Mountains country, he certainly didn't write his most famous poem on that spot. Most of his writing was done in Philadelphia at that time, they would note, and so the only connection Ravens' Knob could have with Poe's "Raven" is that it may have inspired him to write the poem when he returned to the City of Brotherly Love.

On the other hand, scholars who have studied the man might contend that the legend about Poe's visit does have some historical facts that support it. Poe's biographers note that he was a romantic, prone to falling in love at the drop of a hat, which would account for the part of the story about his falling in love with Helena Park "at first sight". The same sources also relate that the poet had some wanderlust, taking many trips on a mere whim. If this were true and the possibility of an inheritance arose, then Poe may not have had second thoughts about traveling half way across the state to Potters Mills, where, history also shows, he may indeed have had relatives in the area.

The Poe family connection to Potters Mills was established through General James Potter's daughter Elizabeth, who married James Poe of Franklin County. On her father's death, Elizabeth inherited "six hundred acres of the General's land' lying west of Potters Mills, but her husband must have purchased additional acreage in the Poe Valley area. Poe Creek, which flows through the valley of the same name, got its title, according to local historians, "from Capt. James Poe, son-in-law of General James Potter". [8]

If Edgar Allan Poe did visit Poe Valley in 1839, he may have been moved by his wanderlust to see what lay over the mountains to the north. After conquering the lofty peak now called Big Poe Mountain and crossing through the dark hollows of the Pine Swamp region, a determined hiker would reach Slide Mountain, maybe seven miles from where he started in Poe Valley. It is at the top of that peak that many scenic overlooks are afforded to those who make the climb, and one of those views is at the place called Ravens' Knob. It is a panorama that has enough natural beauty to engender optimistic thoughts in even the most lachrymose individual, and Poe may have come away from here with high hopes. However, just like his ill-fated love affair with the mysterious Helena, any dreams the poet had of an inheritance were destined for disappointment as well.

Edgar Allan Poe's ties to relatives in the Potters Mills area were distant at best, and by 1839 any bonds he might have had with those connections were decades old. If he did come here with high hopes, he must have left them behind when he returned to Philadelphia, for it's doubtful he was significantly rewarded for his troubles. It is perhaps for this reason that his visit, if it occurred, has been omitted from the history books. History does not concern itself with brief side trips of little consequence, even for the most famous person, but legends do not forget, and the persistent tale clinging to the Potters' ancient hostelry is no exception.

Poe, the legend claims, not only stayed at the Potters' stagecoach stop in Potters Mills in 1839, but he also carved his initials on the wall of his room, which, if they were ever located, would go a long way to proving the truth of the legend. However, they've never been found, despite the concerted efforts of the Shollys, owners of the inn in the 1970's. Moreover, all the original guest registers of the old place have either been lost or destroyed. Some of those records were actually burned by one of the hotel's less-farsighted earlier owners, who, it would seem, watched any proof of Poe's visit go up in smoke.

Some might say that that's as far as it goes, and no more can be said about the matter. We should, they would contend, forget the whole thing, and, in the words of Poe's raven, pursue it "nevermore". Others might argue that since the legend exists, then it must be true. Both contentions would be wrong. There actually does seem to be some physical evidence that supports the legend, but the story itself has not been confined to Potters Mills.

Lovers of some of the most rugged and beautiful spots in our mountains would do well to visit Trough Creek Park in Huntingdon County. Formed by Great Trough Creek as it cuts through Terrace Mountain, the park is bounded by Rothrock State Forest and Raystown Lake Recreation Area. One of the most wild and picturesque spots in our entire state, Trough Creek Park is filled with incredible works of nature like the mysterious ice mine, the amazing Balanced Rock, and the beautiful Rainbow Falls of Abbot's Run. Here also are the sheer stone walls known as Raven Rocks, home in an earlier day to large numbers of ravens who found the deep fissures in the rock cliffs to be an appealing annual nesting place until senseless killing drove them away forever. It was actually the sight of these ravens, local legend states, that inspired Edgar Allan Poe to come back, and at this spot write his poem called "The Raven". [9]

The Huntingdon County tale makes no mention of a local mountain beauty that may have captured Poe's fancy at the time, but perhaps she was overshadowed by the memory of the lovely Serena, Countess of Huntingdon, for whom the county takes its name. What the tale about Edgar Allan Poe does relate is that he visited there during the 1820's or 1830's, staying in a stately stone mansion, not far from Raven Rocks. According to Albert Rung, that capable chronicler of the region, the fine place was home to the superintendent of the Old Forge iron mines, an industry that was booming during the time when Poe supposedly came here and discovered the nesting place that inspired his imagination.

Legends tend to float from place to place, and maybe Huntingdon County's Poe/raven story is based on the Potters Mills tale, but the opposite could also be true. No one can say for sure since any solid evidence to support the legend has seemingly faded away, just like the ravens at Raven Rocks in Trough Creek Park and the old guest books at the Potters' hotel. Even the sturdy stone mansion near Raven Rocks where Poe supposedly stayed is gone, submerged under the waters of Raystown Lake. In fact, the last surviving piece of tangible evidence that might be a link with this foggy remnant of the distant past is a table that is hidden in a back room of the vacant Eutaw House.

Perhaps the table is as old as the one-hundred and seventy-five year old building in which it stands, and if that is true, then its condition is not all that surprising. Blackened with an occasional spot where patrons once ignited puddles of whisky in order to test the alcohol content of their drinks, the surface of the old relic is also covered with initials carved into it by bored travelers waiting for the next stage. As curious onlookers glance over the various defacements today their eyes eventually fall on a set of letters on one corner of the table top that were carved in characters bolder than the other inscriptions, At first the initials seem to be the elusive proof that may at last confirm the legend of Poe's visit here, but the letters

EAP

,although intriguing, are not conclusive enough. Someone else with identical initials, or someone who was a fancier of the poet and the legend, could have whittled those same letters into the table top.

So the legend remains as much of a canard as ever; not a very satisfying result for anyone who hopes to resolve the matter once and for all. Even the master's poems don't seem to offer any clues that shed light on the mystery. Although Poe did write a poem entitled "To Helen", about a young girl who he saw "once only, years ago", and who enchanted him with the "poetry of her presence", it was written, so say Poe scholars, about a woman who had shown him much kindness when he was young. [10]

It would certainly seem that Poe would have written some verses about the mysterious Helen of Ravens' Knob if he was as enamored with her as the legend suggests. Since he apparently did not, the story seems to be nothing more than what the Pennsylvania Dutch once called an *alda weiverglawva,* or "old wives tale". [12] But you never know when new evidence might turn up.

While putting the finishing touches on this story, I had the opportunity to interview an elderly gentleman living in Greens Valley, on top of Nittany Mountain above Pleasant Gap. Ninety-two year old Dave Bilger had lived in or near this little alpine valley his entire life, and he had once owned two-hundred acres of mountain ground, including part of the old stage route from Black Hawk to the top of the ridge. Once, with the aid of a metal detector, he found a Colonial penny on the old stage road, possibly from the pocket of one of the jostled stage passengers. Today he proudly shows the penny to visitors who stop by to hear the old man relate interesting episodes of days gone by.

Almost black with age, the coin is about the size of today's quarter. Along one edge is a nick, caused, claims the old gentleman, by being run over by a stagecoach wheel. The date on the penny is either 1793, the same year George Washington was serving his second year as president of the United States, or 1798, the year before he died. Although the coin was minted forty or fifty years prior to Poe's reputed visit to this area, it may have still been in circulation at that time, perhaps even passing through the fingers of the poet himself.

The Eutaw House and its EAP table

(Potters Mills, Centre County)

BIG CATS OF THE BIG WOODS

Embedded in the county histories of the Keystone State are many exciting accounts of how *felis cougar,* also variously known across the commonwealth as the puma, cougar, painter, panther, or mountain lion, was sometimes hunted down by determined Nimrods. However, there are just as many accounts of how the wily felines sometimes turned the tables so that the hunters became the hunted, and when viewed by the person being chased, the ferocious cats may have indeed looked larger than life.

Fortunately we have more than just subjective personal narratives to determine the actual size of the mountain lions that roamed the forests of those times. Naturalists and biologists of that era did record statistics on the panthers that were brought in for the easy bounty money that was offered for the beasts, and those records show that the lions were often as large as our mountaineers claimed.

In his fascinating work entitled *Mammals of Pennsylvania and New Jersey,* published in 1903, naturalist Samuel N. Rhoads states that of all the panthers killed in the United States up to that time, some of the largest "have been killed in Pennsylvania and Louisiana". [1] Hunters in Pennsylvania occasionally shot panthers that were, according to historian W. J.

McKnight, "ten feet from nose to tip of tail" [2], but even though the average panther was somewhat smaller than that, it was still a formidable creature.

Captain Joshua Sabin, veteran of the Revolutionary War and a well-known Susquehanna County hunter, settled on a farm in the Hopbottom country of that county after the conflict with Britain. Here, in what is now Brooklyn Township, he killed, by his own estimate, "five panthers, a number of bears, some seven or eight wolves, and at least two-hundred deer" during the four year period from 1800 to 1803. One of the panthers was shot with a musket, "loaded with eleven buckshot", which Sabin set up near the carcass of a deer that the panther had killed. The big cat had covered the dead deer with leaves, and the wily hunter knew it would return later that night to feast upon its kill. When it did come back as expected, it triggered Sabin's musket, and every shot found its mark. The large feline, according to Sabin's measurements, "measured nine feet in length from his nose to the end of his tail". [3]

A panther measuring "eight feet and a few inches" was killed by wolf hunter Michael Scheffer in Clearfield County about 1823. One day while out checking his wolf traps, Scheffer came to the trunk of a huge tree that had fallen over into a thicket. Deciding to use the tree trunk as a pathway through the dense forest glen, the wolf hunter started across. Part way over he looked down and spied the animal looking up at him. The unarmed pioneer managed to retrieve a good sized "war club", got back on the log, and "with well directed blows knocked the panther's brains out." [4]

In 1857 a panther measuring nine feet two inches, nose tip to tail tip, was shot by a deer hunter in Chapman township of Clinton County. The man who measured this fallen monarch of the forest was amazed, noting that, had he not seen it for himself, he would never have believed "so formidable an animal inhabited our woods." [5]

Many other examples like this could be noted here, but from those already given it's not hard to imagine the fear these mighty beasts must have engendered in the minds of the mountain folks that were their neighbors. However, it wasn't just the accounts of their size that made the big cats seem so formidable. There were also tales of panthers attacking humans, which were regarded as exaggerations by experienced mountain men like Clinton County pioneer hunter Philip Tome, who claimed such stories were "undoubtedly without foundation". [6] No doubt attacks were rare in Tome's time, the late 1700's when there were fewer people encroaching upon the natural habitat of the mountain lion, but as more people settled in the virgin forests of the interior, such encounters would become more commonplace.

The Pennsylvania panthers proved to be a stubborn lot, clinging to their old haunts in the mountains and refusing to be dislodged without a fight. Many were the nights that the early settlers heard the defiant sound of "the painter's cry" from the top of the ridges towering over their humble cabins. And it is from these early times, and even into the first decades of the 1900's, that accounts of people being confronted by the big cats have come down to us, both in the form of episodes recorded in the history books, and in the non-recorded oral traditions that have been passed on through children, to grand children, and to great grand children of the hardy mountaineers who lived in those thrilling times.

Turning first to the historical records, there is an account in Miss Blackman's *History of Susquehanna County* about a panther attacking Mrs. Edmund Stone of Bridgewater Township about 1811. Mrs. Stone had attended a meeting at the "South school-house" and was returning home on horseback, carrying her child in her arms. As she passed through a woods, a panther that was concealed alongside the trail made a mighty leap in an attempt to spring upon the hapless woman and her baby. Fortunately for the mother and infant, the cat must have been an old one or young and inexperienced, it missed its aim and "passed over the horse's head". [7]

Two Lackawanna County men could also "thank their lucky stars" one frosty moonlit night in the fall of 1837 when they were returning home from a country tavern in Wayne County. H. Hollister and a friend were riding in a horse and buggy on what was then called the old "Connecticut road", and around midnight they passed by a vast swampland the early settlers had named the "Shades of Death", due to its bleak and foreboding aspects. Somewhere in this desolate and gloomy stretch the chilling screams of a panther arose from a dense thicket of alder bushes, hemlocks, and mountain laurel alongside the road. The cries were loud enough to startle the most stout-hearted mountaineer, but when the enormous beast sprang onto the road behind them he was so close that the men could hear the dry limbs crack as he emerged from his hiding place.

The eerie silence of the night was temporarily interrupted by the screams of the pursuing beast, the quickening beat of the horse's hooves on the frozen highway, and the rumble of the wagon's wheels as they clattered over the many stones in the road. For eight miles the tawny panther bounded after the speeding buggy, always managing to remain within a "stone's throw" of the frightened horse and men. The horse began to tire as evanescent clouds of vapor, no doubt looking like puffs of smoke as they formed in the cold moonlit night, came more rapidly from its mouth and nostrils. Finally the panther tired also, and the horse was able to out-distance it, allowing the men to reach the relative safety of the spot known as Little Meadows. It was an unforgettable experience, and the screams of the beast left a permanent impression on the minds of the two travelers. The sounds were so "distinct and appalling", they noted, that they had no further desire to ever encounter another panther. [8]

Up in Elk County, about 1855, a young man named Ben McClelland had a panther scare that was just as unnerving as that of the two Lackawanna County lads almost twenty years earlier. Ben worked for Sheriff Healey during the winter of 1855-56, and the sheriff sent the young teamster on an errand to Warren, Warren County, with a sled and two horses. The sleigh ride to Warren was uneventful, and his business there was completed quickly enough so that McClelland expected on his return trip to make it as far as Highland in Elk County before nightfall. Here he would spend the night, get an early start the next morning, and make it home the same day.

The trip back took a little longer than Ben had hoped, and the curtains of night seemed to be closing quickly. A few miles north of Highland, at a lonely place that had been named "Panther Hollow" after the beasts that often made it their home, the darkness became complete. Then the horses "spooked". Something alongside the road scared them, and they snorted in fear, galloping away at an uncontrollable pace. Turning around, McClelland was shocked to see a panther bounding after him.

Seemingly afraid of the sled, the panther avoided the road, but this slowed it down as it had to plow through the deep snow along the side. It was still a "neck-to-neck" race to Highland, and although Ben was a hunter, he had no gun with him that night. Finally the cheerful lights in the Townley farmhouse could be seen, and when the Townley's cleared fields were reached the panther gave up the chase.

By this time the runaway horses were spent and lathered, and Ben, it was said, was "almost dead from fright". Early the next morning, the panther, who had been the hunter the previous night, fell victim to a party of local farmers who tracked the big brute and found it near the hollow. Here they killed it, but the story of the big cat's attack and its demise must have only strengthened the reputation of the "Panther Hollow" as a place to avoid at night. [9]

Another wintertime panther scare occurred in Clearfield County about 1903-1904 when a mother and her daughter were pursued by a big cat while on a neighborly mission. Fifty-five years later the daughter remembered the event in a letter to a local hunter, who sent me a copy some twenty years after that:

> When I was a little girl of three or four, my parents lived in Morgan Run, on a place called the old Coffee Place [wrote Rosie Bailor in 1959]. My daddy, Ed Lindenmuth, was the blacksmith at the mines, and my mother was Christ Pool's daughter. He was an old-time lumberman and helped cut a lot of the virgin timber in Elk and Cameron Counties.

One winter my dad butchered a big hog, and my mother did up some of the meat and put it in a basket. She dressed me up good and warm, put me on a sled, and gave me the basket to hold. She had friends at Sanbourne, and intended to give them some of our fresh meat. When she put me on the sled, she put me facing back so the wind wouldn't blow in my face while she hauled me. William Brouse lived about half way to Sanbourne, and on the other side of the road was woods.

A big cat followed us. He went back and forth across the road, and when his head was on one side his tail reached clear across to the other. My mom told me the cat wanted our basket of meat, and told me to kick it out of the sled for the cat. I cried and fought, as I didn't want to give our meat to the cat. At last she told me that if I didn't give the cat the meat it would eat me. It had slapped at me with its big foot and hissed.

When at last I gave the cat the meat, it purred like a big house cat, but much louder and coarser. Since I've grown up, I know now that the big cat was a panther, and that my mother was very much afraid of it. Mother told me that she was afraid every minute it would decide to tackle us. I'm glad now it took the meat instead of mom or me. [10]

Rosie Bailor would go on to become a well-respected hunting guide in the big woods country of Clearfield and Elk Counties that she loved so much, and she would see more panthers in her interesting career, recording each encounter in her "personal experience book of contact with animals". But although on several occasions she got close enough to a big cat "to feel its hot breath in my face", Rosie never killed a panther. Either the clever beasts were too quick and got away before she could shoot them, or she was never armed when they did cross her path, but the hide of a Pennsylvania lion never adorned Rosie's hunting lodge on Sander's Run.

Most hunters would just say that such trophies were hard to come by, even fifty years ago, but there were probably other Nimrods around that time that might have expressed a different opinion. The more superstitious outdoorsmen might have recalled the panther over in Lycoming County that killed a doctor near English Center around 1896 (Which is the date on the monument that stands along the roadside near English Center today – see the author's *Pennsylvania Fireside Tales – Volume III.* Rhoads, in his *Mammals of Pennsylvania and New Jersey,* says the date was about 1840).

The incident in question involved a young country doctor named Frederick Reinwald, who practiced in Liberty Corners, Tioga County. One winter day the doctor received a message that he was urgently needed in English Center, Lycoming County. The distance being only about five miles, Reinwald did not hesitate. Picking up his medicine bag and a double-barreled rifle for protection, the good doctor mounted his horse and set off for English Center. As the hours passed and the last rays of daylight finally faded into the lead-gray skies of winter, people in Liberty Corners became concerned. The doctor had not returned when expected, and a heavy snow had begun to fall.

A search party finally went out to look for the missing medical man, but the deep drifts made the task a long and difficult one. Two weeks later his body was found beside a large butternut tree, where, it was evident, he had been attacked and killed by a panther. The doctor apparently hadn't gone out without a fight, as one barrel of his gun had been discharged. He had also attempted to fire the second barrel, but it had misfired. It was concluded by the searchers that the doctor had seen the panther on an overhanging limb of the big butternut and had shot it. In a pain-induced rage, the wounded panther then "sprang from the limb upon the unfortunate man". [11]

Superstition still ruled the minds of many of the Pennsylvania Dutchman in this section of the mountains known as the "Block-House Country" in those times. The misguided beliefs and legends of the original German pioneers who had built the log "block-house" as a protection from Indians would prove almost as hard to down as the Indians had been, and the men who found "Doc" Reinwald's body thought there was something strange about the whole affair.

It would not have taken much of a marksman to kill such a large and well-exposed animal with one shot at such a close range, yet the doctor had failed to do so; and when he attempted to shoot again, his gun misfired. This was a scenario all too familiar to some of the men. Witches could bewitch animals so they could not be shot, or "take the fire" from a man's gun, so as to render it harmless, and, they concluded, this must have been the case here.

The following winter two deer hunters spotted panther tracks in the mountains above Liberty Corners. Jacob Sechrist and Mr. Messner had known Frederick Reinwald, and had considered him a friend. It was, they felt, their duty to avenge the doctor's death in any way they could, and so they talked about what to do next. Agreeing that the panther was probably under the spell of a witch, the two hunters returned home to make the necessary preparations for a protracted hunt.

The next morning they returned to the spot where they had found the panther's tracks. With them they had provisions to last for several days, and each man also carried a "witch-proof" rifle, loaded with a musket ball made of pure silver, which, they believed, was the only sure remedy to counteract the spell a witch had placed upon an animal.

For three days and nights the determined hunters trailed the panther, sleeping on snow-covered ground when night came. On the fourth day they caught up to the big cat in Sullivan County. There, east of Loyalsock Creek, on the mountain near Hillsgrove, they were able to get a clear shot at the elusive lion. When they skinned it, they found a grisly reminder of their friend. In the shoulder of the beast was a rifle ball, which, they concluded, was probably Doctor Reinwald's. [11]

History doesn't go on to say what the men did with the dead panther, but they were probably satisfied to tell all the doctor's friends that they had avenged his death, despite the best efforts of a witch to prevent them from doing so, and that there was now one less big cat roaming the big woods of northern Pennsylvania.

The Reinwald Monument
with English Center Bed & Breakfast in the background
(near English Center, Lycoming County)

THE BEAVER DAM WITCH

At the foot of the eastern terminus of Egg Hill in Gregg Township, Centre County, where the cool waters of Sinking Creek flow into those of Penns Creek, there are many ideal locations for water-powered mills. Shrewd early settlers in the area were quick to realize the business opportunities the waters afforded, and so here, in the shadow of Egg Hill, many mills were eventually erected, including a saw mill and a grist mill which were built by 1793. It was the prevalence of these mills, along with the discovery of many natural springs in the area, that suggested the name for the town which grew up at this site. Today there are no mills left in the tiny hamlet of Spring Mills, but its name reminds us of the time when there were, thereby serving as a link to the past.

It's the history behind the names, the human interest side of that history in particular, that makes the study of place names so interesting. In the case of the mountain above Spring Mills, for example, elderly locals claimed that the first German settlers here named the little ridge *Oie Holle,* which, when translated into English, means Egg Hill. Lifelong valley resident Clarence Musser, born in 1884, told me in 1971 that the original settlers here came up with that name because they found so many wild turkey nests filled with eggs all over the mountain; a fact not well-known anymore today.

That's the case with many of the names of creeks, valleys, mountains, and small towns in Pennsylvania; the origins of their quaint names have almost been forgotten over time, and that, in itself, is enough reason to include a chapter on this subject in a future volume of the *Pennsylvania Fireside Tales* series. However, the topic is discussed here only as an opportunity to mention the quaint little settlement of Beaver Dam, which lies along the "crick" road, as locals would say, about two miles southeast of Spring Mills.

Beaver Dam, as might be guessed, was so named because the first settlers in the area found that a colony of beavers had arrived here first. Attracted to the pure deep waters of Penns Creek, the busy little animals constructed a huge dam of mud and branches that must have been quite impressive. It was at least noteworthy enough that people decided to use the name when referring to the spot, and so the beavers' edifice must have become one of the landmarks people mentioned when attempting to give directions to those unfamiliar to the area. But time and the elements have a way of erasing even the most magnificent natural wonders, and nature didn't hold back when it unleashed its inexorable forces upon the beaver dam.

The beavers, for whatever their reason, abandoned their construction project, and eventually it collapsed, or was ripped apart by human hands, all final traces probably washing away in one of the many spring floods that were once so common in the mountains. But the disappearance of this remarkable structure didn't erase its memory from the minds of the local populace, and although it was gone it was not forgotten, the name Beaver Dam still being used as the name for this locale today. And just as the name Spring Mills recalls the mills that once stood there, the name Beaver Dam reminds us of the landmark that once spanned the waters at this spot.

Unless they make a concerted attempt to look for the place, most people today most likely might think that there is no longer anyone living at Beaver Dam, that it is only an abandoned site or ghost town. That would not be true, and there are no ghosts that haunt the immediate area, at least none that I've been told about. However, Beaver Dam did once have its witch, but that's a story that was almost swept away in the currents of time; almost as forgotten as the little hamlet itself.

Along the back road linking the villages of Spring Mills and Coburn in Centre County, and almost completely hidden among the trees that shade the northern edge of Penns Creek, the little cluster of houses that comprises the village of Beaver Dam sits well off the beaten path. It is a place that is easily overlooked by the passing motorist, and although its location accounts for some of this oversight, the scenery here is probably the main reason that the eyes of passersby are diverted in other directions instead of toward the other side of the creek.

Lovers of the quaint corners and by-ways of the Pennsylvania mountains should add this “stretch” of the Penns Creek Road to their list of trips to take some weekend when wanderlust strikes. The scenery along this little-traveled country highway is beautiful at any time of the year, with either the impressive heights of First Mountain to the south or Egg Hill to the west always within view; but the trip should preferably be taken in the fall after the leaves have put on their autumn colors.

It is during this season that the senses seem more attuned to the past, and so it is this time of year when thoughts might turn to what life around Beaver Dam must have been like a hundred years ago. This is especially true for those who appreciate the few remaining relatively unspoiled sections of the state and the legends they still harbor. For these lovers of “quaint and forgotten lore”, questions naturally come to mind concerning what human episodes, tales, and legends of the long ago might still be heard here. However, to feel the full affect of this place, and to get a real yearning for its legends, the visit should be made in the month of October; the month of ghosts, goblins, and witches.

By the time the “Gay Nineties” rolled around, the citizens of Beaver Dam and the surrounding countryside were used to hearing the shriek of the steam engine’s whistle and the sounds of boxcars clattering along steel tracks. It had been about twenty years since the Lewisburg, Centre, and Spruce Creek Railroad laid down its rails along Penns Creek in 1877, and by this time the area's residents must have thought they had entered the modern age; that a new order of things had finally arrived, and that old ways were fading rapidly into the past. Although that may have been true in most respects, there were certain aspects of life that were slow to change, and among those were the ancient superstitions and beliefs that were brought here from the "Old Country".

Included in these deep-seated beliefs was a strong attachment to the ideas concerning witchcraft. In this respect Beaver Dam was no different than neighboring communities in those days. Each one could lay claim to its share of witches, both good ones, known as *brauchers*, and bad types, often called *hexes*, and each town had at least one sorcerer or sorceress that seemed to be more infamous than the other local witches. In Beaver Dam's case there was the *hex* they called Amanda. Her last name is no longer remembered, other than the fact that it "was a common name like Smith" [1], but the people who lived near her all regarded her with some suspicion. She was, many claimed, a *hex*, though none could prove it. But there were ways that could be used to do so, or so claimed the pundits who knew about such matters. So one day a group of young ladies, their curiosity strained to the limit, decided they would take matters into their own hands.

Living in, or close to, the little village of Beaver Dam in the last years of the 1890's was a family named Evert. Julia Dunlap Evert and her husband John had six sons and six daughters, and the daughters were curious about the neighbor lady who often came to sit and sew with their mother. Amanda and her daughter Mary seemed like normal folks, but Amanda had a darker side, or so claimed the local gossips, and the Evert sisters, Alice, Julia, Verna, Bertha, Minnie, and Lydia, decided to observe her carefully every time she came for a visit.

A common belief of those times was that a witch would not step over a broom. This idea must have seemed incongruous to some when it was recalled that in addition to boiling cauldrons, black cats, and ancient tomes of malicious incantations, a broom was just as important to practitioners of the "black arts" as the Bible was to those who used it to counteract a *hex's* spells. In the witch's case, it was the broom that could sometimes be used like a huge magic wand of sorts when conjuring the weather, and it was also the broom that afforded her a means of transportation. Stories of witches riding their brooms were favorite tales around Halloween, and pictures of an old hag flying through the air atop her broomstick are still common decorations that can be seen during October today.

Rather than question the obvious paradox of the broom's utility to the witch on the one hand and her aversion to it on the other, the Evert sisters, whose curiosity was strained to the limit and could be contained no longer, decided to put the broom test to good use one day when Amanda and her daughter Mary came to sew. Sometime after the visitors arrived, the curious Evert girls took a broom and placed it where Amanda would have to step across it when leaving the house. No doubt the minutes must have seemed like hours as the afternoon passed, and the sisters' emotions probably swung back and forth between excitement and fear while they waited for their mother's guests to leave. But the time finally came.

"Well, it was towards evening and time to go home, recalled Alice Evert's daughter, who had heard the tale from her mother.

"And Amanda said to her daughter, 'Come on Mary', she said, 'we have to get home and take care of supper.'

"And she started to the door and saw the broomstick. And she wouldn't step over; so they assumed she was a witch!"

The broom episode must have inspired the Evert sisters to keep an even closer watch on their mysterious neighbor whenever she came to sew, and on another occasion they saw her doing something, they claimed, that was even more damning than her failure to step over a broom.

"My grandmother and them had an out-building where they kept stuff," continued Alice's daughter.

"And she said for one of the kids to go get milk. 'We're out of milk'.

"And Amanda said, 'Oh no you're not!'

"And the kids saw her in the kitchen take a tea towel and knead it like she was milking a cow. And she got milk!

"They went around telling this story to other people, and there was a young lady who decided she would like to be a witch too, if you can do things like that."

The witch-wannabe was serious about pursuing her dreams, and so she contacted Amanda's daughter Mary, asking her to ask her mother what a person who wanted to be a witch had to do to become one.

"The girl told her mother," continued our story-teller, "and Amanda told this young lady to come to her house at midnight on the night of the full moon."

The naïve girl followed the instructions that were passed on to her, and one night when the moon was full and the appointed time had arrived, the time of night popularly known to the old-time mountain folks as "the witching hour" [2], she knocked on Amanda's door.

"She took the young lady to the attic," recalled the woman whose mother had known the participants first-hand.

"There were two big black kettles there, and something was boiling in each one of them. And the witch Amanda said to the young lady, 'You must swear yourself to the devil and renounce God!'

That was more than the nervous girl could stand. Supernatural benefits be damned, she decided on the spot that they were not worth the sacrifices that she would have to make to gain the powers she had thought would be such fun. Probably without as much as a "good night" the frightened novitiate ran out of the house., and into the ghostly light of the full moon, no doubt making it home in record time. It was an experience that she never cared to repeat, and her desire to pursue such aspirations was apparently satisfied, because, noted our storyteller, "she never did become a witch". [1]

The story of the Beaver Dam witch contains several of the most common motifs that could once be found in the lore and legends of witchcraft throughout Pennsylvania. One of the most common of these motifs was the idea that a witch can't step over a broom, and even as late as 1988 I could talk to people who either believed in the idea themselves or who, in their lifetime, had known someone else who did.

"They always said, you know, if you suspected anybody of being a witch, a witch wouldn't step over a broom if you laid a broom down," recalled one lady who classified the belief as just an old superstition, and who didn't know any good stories about such incidents. [3] But another gentleman I interviewed had a different idea about the belief, regarding it as more than just an old tall tale.

"I used to hear granddad talk about that," noted the "ridge runner" who remembered a lot about such matters.

"He said, 'Never step over a broom. It's bad luck to step over a broom', continued the entertaining storyteller.

" Well, I've stepped over a lot of 'em. I don't know what the difference is in steppin' over it, [but] I know they [witches] won't step over a broom. That's one thing they're definitely scared of. They won't step over a broom. I don't know why." [4]

Some decades earlier this same man suspected that two of his neighbors, a husband and wife in Centre County, were witches. The valley where he and his neighbors lived was sparsely populated about that time, and even just thirty years ago this same valley was still relatively unsettled, inhabited mostly by people who had been there all their lives. As a result, there were folks who were about sixty years behind the times when it came to modern ways of thinking, and they liked it that way, even though it meant accusing your neighbor of being a witch.

In this case, the accused, a woman and her husband, had descended from families who had reputations as practitioners of the "black arts", and people thought the couple was still carrying on the tradition. All sorts of sensational stories were circulated about the acts of witchcraft perpetrated by these two people, and in order to prove to himself that the stories were true, the believer in the broom test decided to use it to unmask the witches.

"I tried that when they first said about it, and I didn't believe it!", explained the man who conducted the test.

"Them two people come here, and neither one of 'em would ever step over that broom! I'd lay it there on purpose to see if they'd step over it. They'd never step over the broom. They'd always reach down and pick it up!" [4]

The old couple lived out their entire lives in the same valley, seemingly unconcerned about or unaware of the rumors that accused them of being witches, and today no one there probably even remembers the tales about them anymore (I have not given the name of the valley because the woman is, to the best of my knowledge, still alive and living there yet). "Time heals all wounds", or so claims the old adage, and in this case it was probably true. As the years passed, the accusations about the two reputed witches were gradually forgotten, and the man and his wife were able to live out their lives in peace. However, as some people living around Coburn and Spring Mills today will attest, it's not always that simple.

Spring Mills can boast of a famous *braucher* all its own. There are many stories that still survive about his powers, and the great deal of good he was able to accomplish when he exercised those powers during the first half of the twentieth century. Benny Ripka's name has come up before in previous tales included in the author's *Pennsylvania Fireside Tales* books, and his name will come up again in future volumes. He was considered to be quite the master at removing spells placed on people or on animals by *hexes,* or so many folks thought, and anecdotes about him are still recalled by local residents.

Those same tales also relate that while he was at the business of lifting spells, Benny also could divine the individual who cast the spell in the first place, or so he claimed. However, in at least one case, Benny's divinations caused a family feud that still divides members of that same family today. The family rift that Benny unintentionally spawned arose from his use of the broom test that was thought to be so effective in forcing a witch's hand. The time the incident occurred was during August of 1953.

"My step mother had twin girls, and one twin died," recalled Benny's great granddaughter in 1999.

"Apparently grandpa Ripka was there, and he laid a broom across the door, and he said ' The next person to come in and pick up the broom, there's the one that bewitched and killed the baby!'

"Well, my one aunt went in and picked up the broom! It caused a big family feud, still lasting to this day. A lot of family still don't talk because of that. Grudges carry very deep in the valley!" [5]

I'm sure readers of this volume never imagined that belief in witches and witchcraft lingered in Pennsylvania as long as it did, but such deep-rooted impressions tend to survive, and among those were the connections between witches and broomsticks.

Scholars say that the ancient Teutonic races held the belief that the broom was sacred to their god Odin, and that they also believed him to be the "ruler of the winds" and the composer of the "song of the storm". These same scholars, taking this a step further by blending these two ideas, go on to say that the superstition about witches riding broomsticks may be nothing more than an imaginative personification of "light scudding clouds that pass rapidly across the sky and herald squally weather". [6]

The scholars are probably correct in their analyses; the connections between witches, broomsticks, and weather do have their origins in mans' earliest attempts to explain the weather and its vagaries. In fact the theory might indeed explain the reason why the Delaware Indians' once believed that high winds were portended by clouds they referred to as "witch's brooms" [7]. Apparently the white man's legends eventually intermixed with and colored even the Indians' weather lore.

Despite the logical explanations for such beliefs, there are always "diehards" who cannot change the way they think, and even today we hear of "devil worshipers" who defile churches in their misguided attempts to follow the path of ancient superstition. At least, however, none of them are reported to have tried to ride a broomstick like one "diehard" in Centre County once attempted to do.

Mary Knoffsinger lived in Greens Valley, on top of Nittany Mountain near the village of Pleasant Gap, Centre County, "back in the 1800's". Apparently she possessed some ancient tomes that contained the most potent formulae in a witch's armory, or so she must have thought. Convinced that sources like the *Sixth and Seventh Books of Moses*, and other diabolical tools of *hexerei* were as true as the passages contained in the Bible, this ardent believer one day decided to put the wizardry to a test.

"She made a salve out of three or four kind of weeds or herbs, you know," recalled the life-long Greens Valley native who had heard the tale from his father. "And she got straddle a broom handle and smeared that stuff around the broom handle. She got on the porch roof and said 'Goodbye'. She waved goodbye; she was gonna fly away!" [8]

The ninety-two year old gentleman paused a moment, with the witch straddling her broomstick, and we waited expectantly for him to continue. I had heard a similar tale from Professor Sam Bayard of Penn State University, but had never gotten a chance to ask him follow-up questions about it. He had been given the story down in Greene County when he was collecting folk tunes there during the 1930's, and it's worth repeating here, even though we have to let the Greens Valley witch poised on the edge of her porch roof.

The woman who told Bayard the tale said she "was going to visit a friend", who lived in Monongalia County, West Virginia, just across the Pennsylvania line from the Pennsylvania towns of New Freeport and Brave.

"She was walking along the road and approaching the house," recounted Bayard, recalling the story that the woman had told to him in all seriousness. "There was a fairly high wind, and she saw the person out in the front yard or barnyard close to a shed, and called to her; and instead of answering, the person simply took wing, as it were, or rather flew up over the shed, to the horror of this lady!" [9]

Of course a person's imagination can be very easily fooled into causing them to see things that aren't exactly what they think they are, and probably the most powerful effect the old beliefs in witchcraft had on people was the way they could cloud peoples' thoughts. These types of influences would explain how some of the more sensational parts of the story about the Beaver Dam witch arose. However, in the case of the Greens Valley witch, even the strongest beliefs weren't powerful enough to overcome the force of gravity. The would-be flyer in Greens Valley did indeed become airborne, but, concluded our storyteller, chuckling heartily to himself as he finished his tale, "she jumped off the porch roof and dang near killed herself." [8]

Fleeing From the Witch
Beaver Dam, Centre County

COUNCIL ROCKS

When old-timers used to talk about unsolved mysteries in the western or "upper" end of Brush Valley, Centre County, the conversation inevitably turned to the odd stone fences on Nittany Mountain. They were always a puzzle, even to the oldest valley residents, no matter how far back in a family's generations you cared to go. A number of explanations as to the origins of the fences had been handed down over the decades, but none of them seemed very satisfying or convincing to anyone, except the story that the walls of stone most likely dated back to the time of the very first white settlers in the area.

The fences are not a freak of nature; they were obviously built by the hand of man, but who those men were, or why they erected the maze of stone walls, is still a mystery that may never be solved. Perhaps clues lie hidden beneath one of the large cairns that sit in the midst of the ancient complex, which, to a more imaginative individual, might appear to be the remains of some medieval fortress from the time of King Arthur and his Knights of the Round Table. Visions of Arthurian knights in armor are not consistent with the history of the area, however, and other explanations as to the origins of the ruins must be explored if the truth is to be found. But even though a number of more realistic explanations have been brought forth over the decades, none of these have satisfied the curious either, mainly because they don't really seem to fit with the overall design and location of the entire complex.

The main feature of this interesting yet mysterious spot are the stone fences that were laid out in seemingly random fashion. Although much taller when they were first lifted into place, the mortar-less walls now only appear to be several feet high. However, just like icebergs, where above water you only see about ten percent of the entire mass, the largest part of the Nittany Mountain fences lies buried under ground, covered by leaves and other vegetation that has slowly decayed and built up around them over the years. But the walls are not the only evidence of man's imprint upon this place.

Here also are the cairns, oval piles of rocks that could pass as burial mounds, and shallow wells whose sides were shored up with carefully placed stones. The construction is certainly not the handiwork of Arthurian knights, but if it were located in England, the Nittany Mountain complex might be compared to historic sites like Stonehenge, or other similar ceremonial spots once believed by scholars to have been used by the ancient Druids.

The Nittany Mountain stone fences have not escaped the attention of archeologists. In 1959 a group of them conducted an examination of the area, but the only thing of significance that was unearthed during the "dig" were some bones under a heavy wooden slab beneath one of the cairns. Subsequent analysis revealed the remains to be animal rather than human; not much evidence from which to draw any conclusions, but the archeologists vowed to continue studying the site. However, despite their professed determination, the scholars' efforts were for naught, and today the walls still rest mutely on the mountaintop, refusing to give up the secrets they hide.

The complex is not that hard to see, sitting there on top of Nittany Mountain. It's just a matter of finding and following a route much like the one celebrated by the poet who wrote about hiking "up the airy mountain" and "down a rushy glen". [1] In this case the stream in the "rushy glen" is not always rushing, but it's not hard to follow the streambed all the way up the mountain until you reach the intriguing place of the stone formations. At first you do have to tread carefully around dense thickets of burdock and wild raspberry bushes, and the trail does become rocky as you get up onto the "first bench" of the mountain, but these obstacles are soon forgotten as the stone structures on the mountaintop eventually come into view.

The walls do not form any kind of pattern. They seem to sprawl all over the mountainside, and, in fact, do sit within an area that is several acres in size. Not the type of thing you would expect to find on a relatively remote section of a mountaintop in central Pennsylvania, the stone fences have no doubt surprised more than one hiker or hunter who has stumbled upon them over the years. However, this would not be the only spot on old Mount Nittany that might have elicited this reaction from people who explore the mountain's trails.

Further to the west on the "summer side" of Nittany are piles of rocks that, when encountered for the first time, surprise and mystify hunters and hikers as much as the stone fences further on down the mountain. Towering over the town of Centre Hall that lies just below, the massive piles of stones appear to be ancient watch-towers and the ruins of an old castle, complete with steps, that do indeed seem to be the work of ancient Arthurian knights. However, the true origin of this complex is not that far-fetched or mysterious.

Locals who know about this place refer to it as "Bennie's Fort", and the towers nearby as "Bennie's Towers", but there are fewer and fewer people today that even know the structures exist, much less how they got here. Some have even suggested that the Indians built them, but nothing could be further from the truth since a single man, and a white man at that, was the architect and builder of the whole complex. That subject, however, is for a future story. The only reason it was mentioned here was to introduce the idea that one individual, if he puts his mind and energy into it, can create some very impressive stone structures. This was, in fact, the basis for one of the better-known stories about who might have built the stone fences on the same mountain.

In my youth, without ever hearing why it was referred to in this way, I often heard the older boys call the place "Council Rocks", and some kids even called it "the Indian reservation", but to the generations of valley men who owned the farm just below the fences, it was always the "Old Improvement". The entire complex was built by one man, so their story went. He was an old hermit who decided to make his home here, and, having nothing better to do, built the walls to help pass the time. The legend of the elderly recluse was a popularly accepted explanation for the genesis of the walls at one time, and it seems to be plausible when some of the other theories are considered, like the tale that claims the fences were built by the earliest valley settlers as a place to pen up their horses.

The legend that the stone fences were built by early pioneers as livestock enclosures was, at one time, another widely circulated tale that appeared at last to reveal the identity of the builders of the fences. However, doubts about this theory arise as well when the physical attributes of the fence complex are broadly viewed.

The fences don't form "pens" (unless further archeological digging reveals lower "fences" that have been totally covered over time), and so couldn't have very well been used as corrals. But even if they were intended for that purpose, it seems that they would have been laid out in a more orderly fashion. Then, too, it doesn't seem likely that the earliest settlers would have spent that much time and effort to build corrals of such dimensions (the archeologists found that the original height of the walls was nine feet) when it took almost all their energy merely to survive. These considerations also throw doubt upon the story that the early settlers built the place as an enclosure for their livestock before they temporarily fled from the valley during the time of "the Great Runaway", a flight precipitated by a terrible Indian uprising in the northeastern part of the state in 1778.

Although no one apparently asked them, these "fleeters", as they were sometimes called, may have been able to confirm that the fences on the mountainside were built for another reason than for the purpose of holding their animals. It has been suggested that the massive stone walls were part of a fortress constructed for protection from the Indians, but it seems a bastion of this size would have found its way into the historical record, and it did not. And when neither history nor science offer much help in solving such mysteries, the only other place left to turn to find any clues is the realm of oral history and legend. By turning to this record in this case, we are once again taken back to the time of the earliest valley settlers, and beyond.

I first heard the following tale in 1971 from eighty-seven year old Clarence Musser. Farmer, country school teacher, and lifelong resident of Brush Valley, Centre County, the octogenarian was an enjoyable source of tales of the long ago, and this was one of his most intriguing.

According to the old man, the complex of stone fences on Nittany Mountain was once home to a small band of native Americans, and, as such, was one of the last Indian encampments in Brush Valley or neighboring Penns Valley. The Indians were said to be here when the very first white settlers came into the valley shortly after the end of the Revolutionary War. Interactions between these newcomers and the Indians on the mountain were always peaceful ones, despite the relatively recent period of conflict, and, according to the legend told to Mr. Musser, the two races got along so well that some of those Indians not only were hired as farm workers by the whites, but also eventually participated in some of the settlers' "frolics" and "bees"; cooperative work sessions like barn raisings, log rollings, or corn huskings that were the social events of the times.

Among the Indians who came down off the mountain to socialize with the whites in the valley below was the tribal medicine man, described by Mr. Musser as the "herb doctor". It was at one of these social events, perhaps a husking bee or a stump-pulling frolic, that the "herb doctor" met a valley girl who captured his heart. She was a Heckman, so says the legend, and a daughter of one of the very first pioneer families in this section. Here, in the valley named for its dense undergrowth of crab-apple, thorn, and hazel bushes, she fell in love with, and eventually married, the swarthy brave from the camp of the stone fences.

The legend goes on to relate that the former Indian "herb doctor" took a white man's name, becoming known as "John Heckman", and pursued a white man's way of life as one of the valley's farmers. He also became a father, "and to this day," claimed Mr. Musser, "the descendants of this marriage are still living in the valley". "You can recognize them," he noted, "by their high cheekbones, dark complexions, or other typical Indian features.".[2]

The legend Mr. Musser heard ends with the "herb doctor" being buried in back of a little white country church near the village of Penn Hall., and it seemed like a nice ending to an idyllic love story. However, I subsequently heard from another individual, who claimed the Indian as his ancestor, that the settlers were reluctant to bury a "heathen" Indian in a plot reserved for Christians. According to this man, the church's elders elected instead to lay the Indian to rest just outside their cemetery's boundaries. It seemed like a cruel fate for an Indian who so thoroughly adopted the white man's ways, but after visiting the graveyard I began to think that the story might be based on fact.

Heckman Cemetery is not that hard to find, but it is off the "beaten path". The old burial ground and the small white country church beside it sit alongside a little-traveled country road just south of the village of Penn Hall in Gregg Township, Centre County. The church has only ever been used for funeral services, but it's no doubt seen its share of those over the decades since the cemetery dates back to 1785 and is accorded the honor of being "the oldest burial place" in the township [3]. But despite their long history of use, the church and its cemetery are still well-maintained by the many valley natives whose ancestors lie buried here. Visitors to this "God's half acre" will immediately notice that its caretakers have a love for the spot, an evident pride in the place, and their diligent efforts were apparent to me early one morning in late August when I stopped there to find the grave of the Indian "herb doctor".

It was a morning typical of that time of year when summer is transitioning into early fall. Blankets of white fog cloaked the ground as far as the eye could see, and mists rising off the mountains on the horizon gave them a decidedly blue cast. Drops of dew glistened in the morning sunlight, and on top of a distant chicken "coop" a rooster crowed. Crickets and birds chirped merrily in the fresh morning air, and stalks of corn in the nearby fields were "in tassel", heralding the advent of autumn. Adding more splashes of color to the picture were the wild flowers growing along the roads, in the fields, and among the weeds choking fence rows. Purple flowers of clover, white florets of Queen Anne's Lace, and orange blossoms of Devil's Paintbrush made the overall scene an inspiring sight, even for those not normally inclined to admire such things.

As I methodically inspected each and every tombstone in the cemetery I was accompanied by a number of pigeons that had decided to look for their breakfasts in the dark green grass. I didn't seem to bother them as I walked down the rows of headstones engraved with names like Mosser, Gentzel, and Koch. Names of other Pennsylvania "Dutch" pioneer families of the valley could also be discerned on the weathered grave markers as I inspected each one, but among all the Bresslers, Moyers, Hennichs, Neeses, Hartmans, and Heckmans, I didn't see an inscription that appeared to be that of the Indian who married the Heckman girl.

Many of the markers were engraved with old German script, and this, plus the badly-weathered condition of the stones, didn't help matters. Finally giving up, I looked outside the confines of the cemetery as well, but no lonely grave could be found, and I began to think that maybe the Indian's final resting place hadn't even been marked with a headstone. It wasn't a pleasant image, picturing this fine specimen of humankind lying in an unmarked grave, but I went away comforted somewhat by the thought that even if other valley residents of the time didn't consider it so, at least to his wife the spot where he lay was always hallowed ground.

Over two decades went by before I met someone else who said they were descended from the Indian who married the Heckman girl, and they only knew parts of the legend. However, they said I should talk to their aunt, who had heard the entire legend from her father, who in turn had heard it from an even older resident of the valley. So it was from this woman, on a cold and blustery day in January, that I heard the story of the lone Indian. His origins, as far as the legend can tell, start with a tribe of aborigines that lived somewhere in the Bald Eagle Valley

"This was a legend that's just been handed down over the years," began the valley resident whose ancestral lines could be traced back to the Indian whose life story seems cloaked in mystery. "The tribe was broken up by the whites, and this Indian got away with his life and followed Penns Creek as far as Beaver Dam (see the previous story entitled "The Beaver Dam Witch" for more details about this locale).

"At Beaver Dam the Heckman's found him, and he was ill or just had not had enough food. But anyway, they found him and took him in; and he lived with them for some time. I don't know how long afterward, but they gave him the name Heckman. Later he married one of the Heckman daughters (at the time she was forty and he was twenty years old), and so we, now not exactly our branch of the family, but some of our relatives, are direct descendants of that Indian and the Heckman girl that he married. Her name was Susan, I think, and he was one of the last Indians in this area." [4]

There was another part of this legend that had been handed down through the generations of my informant's family, and another of those family members recalled the story she had heard from her grandmother; a story about one of the children born to this mysterious dusky Indian and his Heckman bride.

"I remember hearing my grandmother say that she had a cousin they called 'Black Lydia'. And the reason they called her 'Black' Lydia was because an Indian, his name was Heckman, he was a hired man on the farm, had married the mother of 'Black Lydia'. I'm not sure he married [her], but he, you know, 'fathered' the farmer's daughter. The story went that he, for whatever the reason, was [separated] from his tribe."

According to the family's records, Lydia was one of thirteen children born to this union, but it is because of her nickname that she is still remembered today and her brothers and sisters are not. The rest of her story has been preserved in the oral history of the valley where she now peacefully rests, untroubled by taunts and nicknames.

"I remember grandma always telling that Lydia used to cry because of her nickname, and because of being teased about her complexion and Indian father," continued the young lady who had heard the story years ago. "Lydia was darker than her cousins, and her line of family all kept the dark complexion." [5]

Although the legend of "Black" Lydia and her descendants was one of the best Indian legends I had collected to date, it still offered no conclusive evidence as to the origins of the stone fences on Nittany Mountain. The two different versions of the "herb doctor" tale seemed to cloud the picture even more, but I had heard the place called "Council Rocks" in my youth, and even some of the older valley residents remembered it being called the "Indian reservation", so it was worth investigating both versions of the "herb doctor" legend as completely as possible to see if I could determine which one, if either, was based on fact. In the end it was amazing what came to light; three interesting and fairly convincing pieces of evidence were eventually captured in the pursuit of the elusive Indian.

The first fact that fell into place came from an early history of Centre County, where it is mentioned that shortly after the Revolutionary War a man named Peter Heckman became one of the first settlers in Gregg Township of Centre County. Even more suggestive was the information that Peter Heckman was the father of eight children, one of whom was a daughter named Susan. [6] Since the villages of Penn Hall and Beaver Dam both lie within Gregg Township, and since both tie into the Indian "herb doctor" legend, it seemed as though things might be falling into place. However, I still hadn't found the Indian's burial spot, and that seemed to be one of the keys to verifying the story. Then one day I got lucky.

"I can show you that grave," offered ninety-four year old Roy Zettle in 1990. [7] I had been told that the old valley native knew about the Heckman girl and Indian medicine man legend, but I had never expected him to lead me to the grave I had been seeking for so long. Yet the old fellow knew exactly where it was, or at least it had been pointed out to him as such when he was younger, and so one fine June afternoon I found myself back in the Heckman Cemetery standing in front of a weathered tombstone that sits in a corner of the burial ground right in back of the church.

The inscription on the stone is hard to read. It looks like the name might be Geo. Heckman, not John Heckman as stated by the legend. There were also birth and death dates on the stone, 2/25/1794 – 5/21/1876, and they did fall within the legend's time frame. However, I wondered how anyone would know the Indian's birth date that accurately if he had grown up outside the white man's world, entering it only as a young man. Nonetheless, it was still nice to find the burial site, if only to note that it really wasn't outside the confines of the cemetery after all.

The evidence supporting the legend was still not very conclusive, but I continued to follow leads whenever they popped up. Then one day I found a third and final clue that took the form of actual medical evidence. It seemed to substantiate once and for all the truth behind at least one part of the tale, and once again it came from a person who claimed they were a descendant of the Indian medicine man who figures so prominently in the old legend.

The woman had a cousin who was a veterinarian. Dave Z. had attended school in Philadelphia, and had graduated from there. It was while taking one of his "vet" courses in the "City of Brotherly Love" that something unusual turned up.

"They were told they had to take each other's blood to have it tested," recalled the lady whose darker skin and high cheekbones might have been a reflection of her Indian ancestor

"The guy that took Dave's blood went to their instructor, and he said, 'There's something wrong. He has different blood.'

"And the [instructor] looked at it and said, 'Dave, where'd you get your Indian blood?'

"They say you can tell a Negro's blood and any of those others; something about the corpuscles, the shape or something that is different. Dave said he never knew it, and when he came home he said something to his dad. And he said, 'Well, yeah, I know something about it, but go ask Uncle Rob; he knows the story!' [8]

Dave did seek out his uncle, and it was from him that he heard the old family story: the legend which now appears to be partly true – at least the part about the Indian marrying the Heckman girl. Although this part of the legend seems strongly rooted in fact, the rest of the story offers very little help in solving the mystery of the stone fences.

What can be said is that in earlier times Indians often climbed high peaks to be closer to their Great Spirit and to "thank him for all the benefits before bestowed, and to pray for a continuance of his favors." [9] There is a nice view out over the valley from the place once called "Council Rocks" and "The Indian Reservation", and there certainly were Indians that left their marks throughout the valley below, the most prominent reminder being their ceremonial place, still called the "Indian Ring", near the village of Penn Hall. But names and pieces of circumstantial evidence do not prove anything either, and it would appear that the secret of the stone fences may lie buried with the old Indian whose love for a settler's daughter was stronger than the cultural boundaries of the times.

FOOTNOTE:

I have to confess that I've been "holding out" a bit on the reader; kind of saving the best for last. Several years after finding the Indian's grave, I was shown a book entitled *The Search for Lost America – The Mysteries of the Stone Ruins* by Salvatore Trento. Much to my amazement I discovered that the stone complex on Nittany Mountain is not that unique after all. Places just like it have been found from Kentucky into northern Canada, and they all have much in common.

As far as can be determined, they were here when the first settlers came to America, but even the Indians couldn't tell them who had built the fences. Always practical, those same settlers often used the stones as building materials and survey reference points. The stone walls, which are the most prominent feature of the sites: are of "dry stone" construction (that is, no mortar of any kind holds them together); can be as long as thirty feet and as high as six; and are usually situated on high bluffs.

Archeological investigations have found no evidence that the complexes were used as burial pits, and so now the theory is that they are "the remains of some unknown type of ceremonialism". [10] Evidence found at some of the sites has led scientists to speculate that the complexes may have been built by ancient Phoenicians as part of their mining operations during the Bronze Age. These Old World travelers were successful navigators, and in their search for copper and other precious metals they just may have been visiting the New World on a regular basis long before Christopher Columbus "discovered" it.

If the archeologists' theories are true, then legend and prehistory seem to have gotten blended or entangled to a rare degree of perfection in the case of Nittany Mountain's "Council Rocks". It just could be that this was a ceremonial spot of religious significance to the race of men that set up the walls in the first place. It could also be true that local Indians found the walls here and also used them for similar purposes. However, unless further archeological evidence sheds more light upon the matter, it appears that the origins of the stone fences will remain another one of those unsolved mysteries of the ages.

Council Rocks (view of one of the many stone walls on Nittany Mountain), and the Indian's grave (Heckman Cemetery, Penn Hall, Centre County)

FROZEN IN TIME

Following the conclusion of the Civil War, in 1865, everyone above the Mason-Dixon Line welcomed victorious troops home with jubilant celebrations. Accompanying that welcome end to the hostilities was a burst of civic pride that spread throughout the north. It seemed as though every little village wanted to have its own monument commemorating the local boys who had gone off to battle. Some of those men had returned as heroes, but others were crushed and buried on battlefields with names like Bull Run, Antietam, Chickamauga, and Gettysburg. It only seemed right to honor these lads who had given the "last full measure" for their country, and even some towns with smaller populations managed to raise the funds necessary to erect impressive memorials to their fallen sons.

Those monuments can still be seen today, standing prominently in town squares or in front of county courthouses; and they have done their job well, keeping alive the memory of those who died to preserve the Union. The impressive memorials are often topped by sculpted figures of the soldiers they commemorate, human forms frozen in time, and some even have an attached bronze plaque or two providing background information and interesting historical details about those statues. Such information will often be sketchy, merely giving a little history of a regiment's war record, including the battles in which it participated, its commanders, and the like, but other times the plaques will also be engraved with a list of the names of the men who served in the regiment. It is this human touch, putting names with the fallen heroes the monument commemorates, which reminds onlookers of the fact that, in the end, conflicts are not about the glory of war but about mans' inhumanity to man.

Although thoughts of war and the heartaches and suffering it can bring are unwelcome topics to consider, there always seems to be a large number of human interest stories that, phoenix-like, arise from the ashes of battle. These are the tales of the men who fought and died in, or lived through, the terrible struggles on the battlefields, and their stories will not be found by merely staring at the monuments erected in their memory. It takes some reading and research to find the human side of a concrete and stone memorial, and a good example of that fact can be found in Driftwood, Cameron County.

The small hamlet of Driftwood is notable for two reasons. One palm of distinction claimed by this little mountain town is that it is near the birthplace of Tom Mix, famous "cowboy" movie star during the era of silent films. Held just outside Driftwood at Mix Run every summer, the annual Tom Mix Festival still draws people to this remote mountain retreat (one such festival was in full swing when my wife and I passed through here during the summer of 1999), but the village's other "claim to fame", the Civil War monument that stands in the town square, attracts tourists as well.

Mounted on the base of this quaint memorial is a statue of a young man with a broad-brimmed hat on his head and a rifle in his hands. At first the monument appears to be just like any other of its kind, but a closer look reveals that the hat has an adornment that was sculpted along with it, and it's that little decoration that provides the clue to the story behind the monument and the regiment it commemorates: the young soldiers from the Black Forest country of northern Pennsylvania.

Colonel Thomas L. Kane's company of Civil War volunteers consisted of recruits from the counties of Cameron, Elk, and McKean. In the spring of 1861 these rugged and robust young men were given a rousing send-off at Driftwood, from which place the regiment mounted log rafts they had built themselves, poling them down Sinnemahoning Creek until they reached the Susquehanna at Lock Haven. Here they boarded a train to Harrisburg, where they were mustered into service. It was a unique effort by any estimate, and it was said that this patriotic *tour de force*, coupled with their *unique uniforms*, "tended to make their entrance into the war more picturesque than that of any similar body of men in the great conflict". [1]

The new Federal soldiers were hardy backwoodsmen and accomplished riflemen, having grown up hunting the many deer that lived in the thick forests of Pennsylvania's north woods. To a man, they had slain at least one big stag that roamed these same forests, and from this common background came the idea for the regiment's symbol: a buck's tail attached to their hats. It was this decoration that also suggested a name for the company, and so they became known as the Bucktail Regiment of the Pennsylvania Reserve Corps.

Almost all of the "Bucktails" were exceptional marksmen, and so many of them, at one time or another during their enlistment, got their chance to do some "sharpshooting" for the Union army. However, the one outstanding characteristic of each man in the regiment was the buck's tail attached to his headgear, and so the monument in Driftwood, with its soldier wearing a cap adorned by a buck's tail, is absolutely true to life.

There is often an appealing human interest story behind any monument if the matter is pursued far enough, and so it should come as no surprise to the reader that many such tales might be found at Gettysburg in Adams County. There are probably more stone memorials per acre in Gettysburg National Military Park than in any other comparable piece of real estate in the world. Although some of the more interesting episodes linked to these monuments have been captured in print, many have not, and it is a few of these unrecorded annals that will be mentioned in this chapter. Moreover, in some cases stories are still told of unusual events and heroic deeds that occurred during this great battle which seem worthy of a monument of some sort, but which, for one reason or another, were never accorded that honor. Certainly one such tale that would have to be included in this latter category is that of a "drinking party" attended by opposing forces on the night of July second.

Visitors to the battlefield at Gettysburg often pass by the foot of a small battlefield hillock called Culp's Hill without even giving a moment's notice to the little spring nearby. After viewing the other monuments in the park, people can hardly be blamed for breezing by the hollow half-shell of stones and concrete that serves as a partial covering for the waters that bubble up to the surface at this spot. However, a closer look at the stone canopy reveals a nameplate fastened to it, and on the nameplate are the words "Spangler's Spring". It was here, at this quiet little fountain, that something so implausable happened after the second day's fighting that for many years after the battle historians and other scholars believed it was only a tall-tale, invented by someone with a vivid imagination.

The hot "dog days" of July could hardly be the time anyone would pick to engage in a battle, but on July first through third of 1863, soldiers of the Blue and the Gray contested the fields of Gettysburg. The peaceful rolling hills of Adams County, baked by the hot sun of summer, were rapidly turned into dusty infernos by thundering instruments of warfare, and at the end of every day soldiers' thoughts turned to thanking God for still being alive, filling empty stomachs, resting weary bodies, and slaking parched throats.

As night settled over the battlefield around Culp's Hill on the evening of July second, men in blue and gray uniforms spotted the inviting spring located between the front lines of the opposing armies. Decades later aging veterans would fondly recall what happened next at the spring, but for many years historians tended to ignore them, refusing to accept that their memory of a "drinking party" on that hot evening in July was anything but a tall-tale. But the feisty old vets insisted that the story was a true one; that soldiers from the North and from the South had gathered together at the spring to slake their thirsts. Only hours before these same combatants had been trying to kill one another, but now they put aside their hostilities to exchange greetings. Drinking in peace from the same waters, the erstwhile foes even waited in turn to fill their canteens so they would have water to take into battle against each other the very next day. [2]

Stories of the "drinking party" at Spangler's Spring were told and retold at every Gettysburg reunion of the Blue and the Gray until infirmities and the "Grim Reaper" kept the old soldiers apart, and after their voices were heard no more, the legend of Spangler's Spring was forgotten or relegated to the status of a canard. In fact, it wasn't until almost exactly fifty years later, during yet another great war, that a similar episode breathed new life into the story and perhaps convinced many skeptics that the drinking party at Spangler's Spring was no tall-tale after all.

The First World War was even more horrible in many respects than the Civil War. But with its horrors of trench warfare, poison gas, sub-machine guns, and other "improved" methods of mass destruction, the great European conflict still could not stifle the desire for peace that dwells in every decent human being's heart, especially on a special December day. In letters to home, the soldiers of both the German and British armies recalled the "astounding" events that occurred on a battlefield in France during December 25th ,1914, the first Christmas of the First World War.

It seems that when Christmas came to the trenches of the opposing armies that day, it brought with it a complete cease-fire; a truce that was honored as completely as any formal declarations drawn up in the Articles of Surrender four years later. In some cases the Germans started the festivities, lighting candles on Christmas trees they had placed on the parapets over their trenches. In other places the British troops took the lead, igniting bonfires and setting off explosions to usher in the holiday.

Much to the chagrin of the commanding officers, the good will tended to spread across the "no man's land" between opposing trenches no more than a few hundred yards apart, and men from both sides were soon shaking hands, exchanging addresses, and singing carols to one another. In one case it was recalled that the enemy troops even formed teams and competed in a soccer game on a field decorated with strands of barbed wire and pockmarked with shell holes.

Officers in the British high command would later issue orders forbidding any such fraternization with the enemy again, but the "Christmas truce", as it would later be called, was an extraordinary event, one that Sir Arthur Conan Doyle, creator of fictional detective Sherlock Holmes and an historian of the

"Great War", would later call "one human episode amid all the atrocities". [3]

The "Christmas truce" of the First World War would seem to leave little doubt that the terrible clash of armies at Gettysburg during the Civil War could have led to some strange "bed fellows", including the fraternization of opposing armies at Spangler's Spring following the second day's battle. However, there is yet another remembrance of odd events during the struggle at Gettysburg that, if true, also supports the idea that an event like the drinking party at Spangler's Spring could have actually happened. This other episode, which scholars would also no doubt label as apocryphal, supposedly occurred after the second day's battle at a colossal collection of boulders called Devil's Den.

South of Gettysburg, near the small eminence called Little Round Top, regiments from the opposing forces clashed on the afternoon of July second . Ragged lines of men, attacking and counter-attacking one another in separate skirmishes across the line of battle, would later remember the hand-to-hand fighting with bayonets and musket butts that raged in the Peach Orchard that day. Other combatants would recall the trampled and blood-soaked stocks of grain in the Wheatfield where Northerners and Southerners, not more than thirty yards apart, blasted away at each other with deadly effect. Near the Wheatfield, at the place called Devil's Den, Confederate snipers battered by Yankee artillery fire could later attest that, during that afternoon at least, this place on the battlefield was one of the most God-forsaken places on earth.

As the evening of July second crept onto the battlefield, the constant rattle of musket fire and the deafening roar of the cannons that had lasted all day finally stopped. This eerie silence seemed to be a signal for the dense smog of dust and gun smoke that hung over the area to fade away with the last rays of sunlight. Like cowardly ghosts, the clouds that had choked the war zone evaporated into the night, and tired and wounded soldiers, whose emotions had alternated between rage and terror during the day, now thought only of a good night's rest, a decent meal, and liquid refreshment. Over on the Wheatfield the groans and cries of wounded and dying soldiers filled the night, and among the most plaintive calls were the pleas for water.

Among the most-severely wounded combatants were those whose limbs had been lost during the battle. Limb-less men were not uncommon at Gettysburg, either because surgeons often had no other choice except to amputate arms or legs where bones had been shattered by musket balls, or because a man's appendages had been blown cleanly off by an exploding artillery shell. Out on the Wheatfield this night there were "amputees" whose limbs had been separated from their bodies that day by battlefield explosions rather than by a surgeon's saw.

Some of the limb-less survivors of the terrible clash at the Wheatfield were armless, while others had only stumps where their legs had been, and the hope that there would be a

Good Samaritan to bring them water must have faded in these "amputees' " minds as darkness claimed the battlefield. There would be no one to come to their aid, and their thoughts turned to the nearby spring that they recalled seeing over at the place called the Devil's Den. Although hidden from view today, the spring was out in the open during the time of the battle. It was this spring, if we can believe another historically-unsubstantiated tale of the battle, that prompted the armless and legless men at the Wheatfield to take desperate measures.

"There are plenty of anecdotes on the Battle of Gettysburg," noted the retired battlefield guide, "but the one I like best of all is called 'piecing up'; it happened out at the Wheatfield. The men without arms carried the men without legs to get water at Devil's Den. I read it in a little pamphlet put out by the Philadelphia and Reading Railroad. Everybody thinks I'm cracking up; the more you talk about it the more silly it becomes, but it was true in my opinion". [4]

One thing that has been well documented about the terrible casualties at Gettysburg is the fact that the number of men who lost appendages during the battle was astounding. First-hand reports by those who were there recount how surgeons amputated so many limbs that piles of arms and legs accumulated outside the battlefield surgery tents. Visitors to the battlefield on the first days following the conflict here were likewise sickened and appalled by the many arms and legs that "could be readily seen littering the fields and woods". [5]

Although men were most often the victims of the Gettysburg bloodbath, there were many animals that also never survived. Countless horses and mules were killed and wounded here, and it is said that hundreds were buried near Spangler's Spring. And although it was an infrequent occurrence, mans' best friend was sometimes struck down as well. Several strays were taken in as pets by units on both sides, and some of these courageous little curs were shot as they charged into battle with their soldier friends.

If anyone has doubts that there were dogs with the troops at Gettysburg, they should visit the memorial to the Eleventh Pennsylvania on Doubleday Avenue. Here, at this monument on the hallowed fields of battle, they will see the elevated statue of a Union soldier presenting arms, but a lower look will then reveal the figure of a dog, sculpted from a coal black block of granite and lying on a little shelf at the foot of the young warrior. There's no inscription to tell the onlooker why the dog's figure is there, or what the canine's name might be, but therein lies another of those human interest tales that often cling to monuments of fallen heroes.

There's really no great unsolved mystery behind the identity of the dog on the monument dedicated to the Eleventh Pennsylvania. In fact, the reader has probably already guessed that she was the mascot of the regiment, and that's exactly who she was. "Sally", or "Sally the war dog", as historians would later call her, was indeed a battle hound. By the time the armies of the

North and South clashed at Gettysburg Sally had developed some distinctive traits; likes and dislikes that were strongly reinforced from being in the company of Union soldiers for so long. It was her ingrained loyalties that endeared Sally to the troops who took her along with them wherever they went, and it was said that Sally had three "pet hates".

"She hated Confederates, naturally; she was a Union dog. What'ya expect!", recalled the battlefield historian one day when he told us some of the legends of the monuments at Gettysburg.

Sally's second "pet hate", the historian went on to explain, was civilians, "because she was a soldier's dog", with her third hate being women; "because she was a man's dog"! [4]

Sally the war dog survived the Battle of Gettysburg, but the faithful little terrier was later "killed in action" in Virginia at the Battle of Hatcher's Run. After being given a ceremony that included "all the honors of war", she was laid to rest on that same battlefield. [6]

There is at least one other monument at Gettysburg that has a dog on it, and that's the monument to the "Irish Brigade", which features a big Celtic cross and an Irish Wolfhound as its main components. In that case, however, the dog that's depicted on the monument is dedicated to a breed, rather than to one special animal. Without doubt, however, there must have been other "Sallies" at the great Gettysburg conflict during those three fateful days in July, and perhaps their stories would make interesting reading as well. If so, then it's too bad their "biographies" were never recorded for posterity. Nonetheless, there are still plenty of monuments at Gettysburg that provide intriguing entertainment for anyone who delves into the stories behind their façade.

Of course the statues and monuments at Gettysburg were basically erected to memorialize the men who fought and died here. Tourists regularly stream through the battlefield park to see this vast array of memorials, all the while trying to visualize what the terrible struggle must have been like. So intense is the interest that re-enactors and movie producers still come to the park to recreate the drama that unfolded here. It would seem, however, that once in a while imaginations can get out of hand. Take for example the story told about the statue dedicated to Andrew's Sharpshooters, near the Irish Brigade monument.

It seems that a jokester once caused quite a stir in the little town next to the military park. For a period of several weeks, sometime in the first years of the twentieth century when the memory of the clash was not yet that stale in town folks' minds, there were reports that someone was shooting at people who ventured onto the battlefield after dark. That someone, so ran the rumor mill, was the figure on the monument honoring the regiment of sharpshooters from Massachusetts.

The Massachusetts men were called Andrew's Sharpshooters, named after Governor Andrew of the Bay State, and the prankster who chose their monument for scaring people picked his site well. Depicted on the face of the monument is the profile of an erect sharpshooter, carefully taking aim with his musket. A superstitious person, passing by here on a particularly dark night might have been scared out of his wits when a shot rang out, apparently from the rifleman on the monument. Meanwhile, the "little devil" hiding behind the memorial was probably trying to stifle his laughter so as to remain undetected.[7]

The story of the shooting statue of Gettysburg no doubt evolved because of a hoax perpetrated by someone who liked to fool people, but if someone actually thought the statue could shoot at them, then they should have also considered the fanciful reasons it might have been doing so. Ideas that come to mind might be the statue's dissatisfaction with its placement on the battlefield, its size, or the direction it's facing. All might be reasons a statue, if imbued with a life force, would be upset, but in the end it would have to be content with its lot, realizing that it was an honor just to be there in the first place.

It didn't require a whole lot of searching to uncover the story of a real live person whose long-departed spirit might be forgiven if it were still upset about not having a statue honoring its contributions toward victory at Gettysburg. This unsung hero, one who might be called Pennsylvania's own "Paul Revere of the Civil War", was never accorded any credit for his brave deed except for passing references in old newspaper accounts and in an obscure history of the great battle.

When General Robert E. Lee's Confederate forces marched upon Chambersburg, in the latter part of June, 1863, they cut down telegraph lines to prevent news of their invasion. Union loyalists in the town knew that word of the attack must get to Governor Curtain in Harrisburg so he could mobilize a response, and so they asked for a volunteer to carry the knowledge of Lee's location and troop strength to the state capital.

Ben Huber, one of Franklin County's "country lads", decided to accept the challenge, and set off through the mountains. His route took him through the "Three Square Hollow Gap", near the present-day village of Blain, then to the villages of Loysville and New Bloomfield. At Newport the young rider caught the Penn Central express train to Harrisburg, where he passed on the vital facts to the governor, who in turn passed them to General Meade. Meade then turned his forces toward Gettysburg, and the rest is history. [8]

There are more accounts, like that of Ben Huber's, that could be related here, but if all of Pennsylvania's unsung heroes of the great Civil War were immortalized by statues in their honor, then the landscape might begin to look a bit cluttered. Perhaps the best we can do for these people is to appreciate and publicize the legends and tales of their valor and sacrifice. After all , Civil War heroes whose faces and deeds have been frozen in time by the hands of gifted sculptors have already achieved some degree of immortality, and other less-famous heroes deserve no less.

The Bucktail Monument (Driftwood, Cameron County)
And Monument to the 11th Pennsylvania with Sally the War Dog
(Gettysburg National Military Park, Gettysburg, Adams County)

Close up of Sally the War Dog statue on the 11th Pennsylvania monument, and original photo of Sally used by the sculptor as a model for the statue. (Photo courtesy of Division of Archives and Manuscripts, Pennsylvania Historical and Museum Commission; "Military: Civil War: Sally the War Dog"; MG218 Photo Collection)

Monument to the Andrew Sharpshooters

(Gettysburg National Military Park, Gettysburg, Adams County)

SPITZBUBEN

Englishmen preferred to call them "highwaymen", but the Pennsylvania Dutchman used a more colorful term, referring to these "knights of the road" as *Spitzbuben,* which when translated into English meant rogues or thieves.[1] In the early to mid 1800's tales of such miscreants were once quite common throughout the Keystone State, and oral accounts of the *Spitzbuben* from that earlier time might be heard yet today if the seeker is fortunate enough to find the right person. Those sources of the old tales are disappearing rapidly, however, and in another ten or twenty years their voices will be silent and their stories heard no more. Death "the Harvester" will then have robbed us all, just as callously as the highwaymen who once plied their trade along the lonely mountain byways of almost every county in Pennsylvania.

In the eastern counties of Berks and Lehigh remembrances about the "Buzzard Gang" or about "the Doanes", two gangs which once terrorized travelers and settlers in that section of the state, are still recalled by the very oldest residents of the Blue Mountains. To the west, in Butler County, a group of horse thieves known as the "Stone House Gang" left their imprint upon that region during the 1840's and 1850's. The midsection of the state, on the other hand, appears to have been a place preferred by solitary highwaymen or by those working in pairs or threes rather than in large gangs. Here, where the Allegheny and Appalachian Mountains form countless secluded gaps and shadowy glens, ideal hiding places for a highwayman waiting to ambush an unsuspecting traveler, stories of some of these lone bandits could still be heard just ten years ago.

Sometimes in these oral accounts the roadside thieves are portrayed as debonair and handsome, while at other times they are described as coarse and ill-favored, but without exception the purpose of their escapades was always the same: to get rich at someone else's expense. Wealth was hard to come by in those halcyon days of the mid-1800's, and peoples' definition of a rich person was not much different than it was seventy years previously when a man was considered "well off" if he owned "a long-barreled shotgun, a Brungart plow, and a red wamus." [2]

Although a shotgun, a plow, and a warm red jacket were once counted among a farmer's most prized possessions, none of these items were coveted by a highwayman. What the robbers of the road wanted first and foremost was ready cash in the form of gold coins and paper money, and many highwaymen were quite successful in getting fair amounts of each. Some were so consistently successful, in fact, that they became notorious in the process, but no other roadway bandit reached the level of infamy achieved by David Lewis.

'Davy' Lewis was probably the most popular highwayman in Pennsylvania at one time. Born about 1788, Lewis was a relative unknown until he reached his late twenties. Then, in 1815, he began a remarkable one man crime wave that lasted five years and ranged in Pennsylvania from Franklin County in the south to Clearfield County in the north, and from Dauphin County in the east to Bedford County in the west.

"Lewis the robber" was the name bestowed upon him by the general public, but they could have just as well called him "the gray ghost of Penn's Woods" because of the way he seemingly melted back into the forest once he ambushed an unsuspecting traveler on a secluded mountain highway. Although his nefarious exploits included robbery, counterfeiting, prison escapes, and other swash-buckling crimes, and although his name generated feelings of fear in the hearts of many, Lewis was still popularly regarded as somewhat of a hero. It was said that Pennsylvania mountaineers thought of him as the Robin Hood of the hills who "took from the rich and gave to the poor", [3] and stories about his exploits became deeply entrenched in the state's folklore.

Lewis was a remarkable person for a number of reasons, not the least of which was his seeming indifference to danger. The man's audacity became legendary, but he was also noted for a demeanor which seemed at odds with the line of work he chose to follow. Remembered as "very pleasant and agreeable in social conversation and manners", Lewis was also said to be "quite an Adonis" according to an historical account written over sixty years after his death. However, after Lewis died in the

Bellefonte jail in 1820, tales of his prowess and exploits continued to grow and were no doubt embellished until they reached legendary proportions. So the aforementioned historical account, which went on to describe him as someone "of fine figure and physique, with features regular and beautiful", probably contained romanticized exaggerations about the man; details that were once part of the Lewis legend. [3]

Among the favorite legends about Lewis the Robber are the tales of his buried treasure and his "hideouts". He had many such hiding places if the local stories are true, and in some areas the popular belief still prevails that most of his concealed treasures have never been found. Widely-circulated tales in Centre County once popularized the idea that Lewis had concealed some of his ill-gotten gains along Six Mile Run in the Allegheny Mountains north of Port Matilda. Over in Huntingdon County local belief at one time was that Lewis used present-day Indian Caverns as a hideout and had loot stashed near there. Other Huntingdon County tales relate that Lewis hid his stolen money at several spots on top of Tussey Mountain "near the ice caves", marking one of the spots with a stone having a code number carved into it.[4]

David Lewis left his mark behind in another way as well, and that's in the form of the place-names that were assigned to his hideouts by locals who regarded him as a folk hero. David Lewis' Outlook in Bedford County is one such site, and in

Cumberland County treasure hunters can search in at least three spots where Lewis supposedly concealed $100,000 he robbed from a bank in that same county. All three places are "off the beaten path" yet today, and anyone wishing to explore them should be prepared for some strenuous hiking and should have neither a fear of heights nor a case of claustrophobia.

One of these possible Cumberland County treasure spots is a natural cavern on the ridge locals call Cave Hill along the Conodoguinet Creek north of Carlisle. The second, also a subterranean hideaway, is located in the confusing wilds of Doubling Gap; older residents there still refer to it as "Lewis the Robber's Cave".[5] The third place is an impressive "den" of massive stones located on top of the South Mountain in Michaux State Forest. Known as Lewis' Rocks, the hard-to-reach spot contains many "rooms" formed by the jumble of boulders and so it makes an ideal hiding place. It was regarded as Lewis' main base of operations when operating in the Cumberland Valley.

Lewis' memory not only lives on in the places named after him, but also in the folktales that were told about his exploits. The notion was so widely accepted that he was like Robin Hood of Merry Old England or akin to the Rob Roy of Scotland, popularized in Sir Walter Scott's *Waverley Novels,* that people loved to tell and retell the stories that concerned Lewis' "good deeds" and his bravado. Several of these stories still survive, and one that is probably very typical of many others that could once be heard about the man recalls the time when Lewis had a fortune within his grasp and didn't even know it.

General Philip Benner was no fool. The great Revolutionary War officer and astute businessman moved to Centre County after the war, and here he became a successful iron master. The General's trains of pack-horses carried ingots from his forges at Rock Iron Works, near present-day State College, to markets as far west as Pittsburgh, and folktales say that the General even made that trip on horseback himself once. After collecting a large cash payment for ingots his pack trains had carried to the "Iron City", Benner decided to make the trip back home all alone, carrying the money with him.

The general was no doubt feeling very satisfied with his business transactions, and that euphoria probably lulled him into a false sense of security. As he rode along shadowy mountain passages and in and out of lonely glens, he must not have been as attuned to the sounds and dangers of the forest as he should have been. If he had been more alert, the iron master might have sensed the ambush that was set for him around the next bend in the trail, but since his mind was elsewhere, the general was taken off guard when he saw the highwayman pointing a pistol at his breast.

The account goes on to relate that Benner recognized the highwayman as David Lewis and realized that resistance or an escape attempt would be futile. The quick-thinking soldier then thought of another way out of the situation, exclaiming "Oh, Mr. Lewis! You are just the person I was wanting to see. Things have been difficult! We've been having problems in finding enough good ore, and the market is so slow. I desperately need some money!"

What happened next, according to this local account, casts some doubt on whether or not the confrontation ever took place at all. The episode ends with Lewis handing Philip Benner a "sum of money", after which they "proceeded on their respective ways".[6] The story may have been invented by admirers of General Benner to show how cool and quick-witted he could be under fire. On the other hand, the tale could have come from Lewis' admirers as well; those who had heard of the time the soft-hearted bandit helped a widow whose farm was about to be taken from her because she couldn't pay her taxes.

When his profession is considered it doesn't seem likely that Davy Lewis would ever end up "short" on cash, but according to another tale about the famous bandit, Lewis found himself in just such straits one day when he was riding through Centre County. This lack of funds was a state that the outlaw could not tolerate for very long, and his criminal mind quickly considered methods to correct the situation. By the time he came to the next farmhouse in Penns Valley, the clever desperado had thought of a way to rob the occupants. His plan was to ask for change for a five dollar bill, and then watch where their money was hidden.

When he reached the old homestead he dismounted, walked up to the front entrance, and knocked loudly. After some time an old woman opened the weather-beaten door, and, much to his surprise, began to cry when he asked her for change. After composing herself, the farmer's wife explained that they were too poor to change the five dollar bill; that within the hour a constable would arrive to repossess their farm and their only cow. The family's plight touched the heart of the would-be thief, and he produced a twenty dollar bill from his own pocket, telling the woman to use it to pay the constable and make sure she got a receipt when she did so. The mysterious benefactor then melted back into the nearby woods, leaving the woman standing in her doorway scratching her head.

When the ill-tempered constable arrived, his first intention was to evict the family, but when the woman gave him enough money to cover the taxes owed, he could do nothing else but give her the receipt she demanded and ride on to the next place where he had other taxes to collect. From his hiding place in the woods, Davy Lewis had watched the entire proceedings, and the constable had not ridden far before he was looking down the barrel of a pistol. Quicker than it had taken him to get the woman's tax money, the constable handed it over to the highwayman, along with twenty dollars of his own. [6]

Anyone who would rob a constable was not the faint-hearted type, and David Lewis seemed to enjoy toying with and hiding from the men who were trying to capture him. He would, when in jail, joke about such chases, calling them "fox hunts" [3], and one of his favorites would have been the story of the time in Cumberland County when a band of determined vigilantes were so close on his heels that they tracked him down to within ten miles of his hideaway at Lewis' Rocks.

Like many desperados, Lewis seemed to experience a sort of euphoria in risky situations, and so instead of running away, he decided to meet his pursuers in the woods by Pine Grove Furnace on Piney Mountain. The bold robber calmly rode out of the shadows and asked the men if they were hunting someone. The bounty hunters explained they were searching for the notorious highwayman Lewis, and they asked the horseman if he knew him.

"Oh yeah, I know him real well," was the stranger's reply, and for the next two days he rode with them, looking for the elusive bandit. Two months later, so the tale ends, he wrote them a taunting note saying that "The guy you were hunting was the man that was helping you!" [7]

Daring Davy Lewis was successful in avoiding capture for awhile, but one fine June day in 1820 he was wounded during a wild west type shoot out when a posse of pursuers caught up with him and his partner Connelly on the Driftwood Branch of Sinnemahoning Creek, Clearfield County. Both Lewis and Connelly were mortally wounded in the gun fight, Connelly later dying on the Great Island near Lock Haven and Lewis expiring several weeks later in the Bellefonte jail. It should have been a sober lesson for anyone who thought they could defy the law and win, but Lewis' death apparently did not deter others from admiring his successes and following in his footsteps.

A favorite scheme used by any highwayman was to surprise his victim at a lonely spot in the mountains. Such a place not only being a good location for an ambush, but also providing surroundings into which the bandit could readily disappear after he committed his crime. One area that was well-suited for such tactics was the Seven Mountains section of Mifflin and Centre Counties, the notorious Lewis and Connelly themselves lurking here at different times during their infamous crime spree.

Today this vast scenic mountain land, between Milroy, Mifflin County, and Potters Mills, Centre County, is part of the Bald Eagle State Forest and Rothrock State Forest preserves, and as such should rightfully remain in a natural state for generations to come. How many other highwaymen committed crimes in this wild and unsettled area is not recorded, but according to local folktales there was at least one. His story was related to me by an elderly native of the area who heard it directly from the intended victim.

"Now this was a story from 'Cooney' Immel himself," recalled the elderly gentleman whose ninety-four years of living had not dimmed his memory of the many folktales and legends he had heard as a boy. This particular tale of a highwayman in the

Seven mountains, "back in the 1800's", preserves a picture of how these wayside bandits sometimes conducted their business. The thief's intended victim, a mister Immel, was known by the unusual nickname of "Cooney", probably because of his prowess in hunting raccoons.

" 'Coon' Immel used to live in Poe Valley – that's part of the Seven Mountains here," explained our narrator. "He used to peddle shingles to Lewistown. Years ago they knew nothing about sawing shingles; they used to split them out. I suppose you never saw a split shingle, " he continued. "You see, they weren't straight like a shingle. They were sort'a curved in, but yet they were pretty near one thickness too. That's the way they covered the roofs in those days.

"So Cooney went to Lewistown one day with a load of shingles. He'd get twelve dollars for a one-horse load of shingles. On his way back, coming up the Seven Mountains, he seen a fella going alongside the road with two canes. Oh he was awful helpless! Cooney thought he could hardly walk, so he helped him up on the wagon.

"He said it was sorta' moonlight, and after he was on the wagon he seen this fella was turning the bottom off his one cane. So he watched him pretty close. Finally he seen he had a knife blade in the end of the cane, so he knew his intentions. The man knew he was peddling shingles over there, and he was after the money. So Cooney grabbed the cane from him, and the fella jumped off the wagon and run into the brush!" [8]

The highwaymen of yesteryear have faded into the past, with records of their deeds preserved mostly in the form of oral accounts handed down over the years. Perhaps that is why their modern day counterparts still try to get rich at others expense; they haven't learned that crime doesn't pay. Nor have they learned that there is never any rest for those who have committed a crime. The "long arm of the law" is always reaching out for them either until they are apprehended or until they die. But even after death there is no guarantee their souls will find rest; at least if the famous highwayman in the poem of the same name is typical of the breed.

Perhaps, if the realm of folklore and legend is a reliable guide, the old rhyme has some truth to it when it tells of the phantom highwayman that can be seen riding over the dark and lonely moor "when the wind is in the trees, and the moon is a ghostly galleon tossed upon cloudy seas". [9] The ghost of this gunned-down highway bandit, and maybe the restless spirits of other highwaymen like him, are perhaps destined to ride forever, looking for a lost love, bemoaning wasted lives, or searching for their next victims.

Lewis' Rocks

(Michaux State Forest, Cumberland County)

MAIDS OF THE MIST

Sightseers who go to Niagara Falls are always impressed by the small excursion boat that takes riders so close to the roaring cascade that they feel they can almost reach out and touch it. When viewed from above, the powerful little vessel seems to become lost from time to time in the dense mists that rise from the foaming waters of the Niagara River, and that's surely why the owners of the ship have named it the "Maid of the Mist". Without doubt, the little boat has become a favorite attraction at Niagara Falls over the years, but there are Pennsylvania waterfalls and creeks which have their own maids of the mist, and time has not diminished the interest in the old legends about them any more than it has weakened the popularity of the Niagara boat ride

Counted among the most popular legends in the Keystone State are those concerning young Indian princesses who drowned themselves when their fathers refused to let them marry a white man or a warrior from a different tribe. The motif has become a familiar one over the years, finding a home in many different parts of Pennsylvania and supplying the place-names for a lake in Wyoming County, a wild glen in Carbon County, a waterfall in Monroe County, and a creek in Clinton County .

Young Woman's Creek in Clinton County was so named, according to one legend, for a young white female prisoner who was murdered by the Indians and thrown into the creek when she could no longer keep up with her captors. Afterwards, the legend states, the woman's ghost would appear here, materializing in the thick evening mists that tend to collect at the spot where she drowned. It was said that she would always appear whenever any Indians camped there, and if the warriors stayed a second night they would, they said, be "fired upon by unseen faces". [1] There is, however, another legend that preserves a different explanation for the stream's odd name. It's an account that was once familiar to many older citizens of the area, and one they claimed held the true explanation for the naming of the stream and for the Indian town that once sat where the creek empties into the West Branch of the Susquehanna River.

When the first white settlers entered this section of the state they were told by the Indians living here that they called the stream "Young Woman's Creek", and that their village was named "Young Woman's Town". The taciturn natives apparently were unwilling to give the settlers a definite account explaining the origin of the name, and perhaps that's why the white man eventually discarded the title of the town in favor of their own.

After the Indians' abandoned their village and white men's cabins took its place, the name "Young Woman's Town" was eventually replaced by the more geographically descriptive title of North Bend, which reflects the way the river "bends" at this spot, and that's what the town is called yet today. However for some reason the whites decided to keep the Indians' name for the nearby creek, translating it into to their own language. Perhaps the white men decided to assign a name to the creek that recalled the Indian name because they liked the mystery behind it, but maybe the designation was preserved because it reminded them of the unusual love story that was said to have come to its conclusion on the banks of the swift-flowing creek that meanders through what today is Sproul State Forest.

At one time, according to this second legend, there was apparently a small band of Indians living in the mountains near where North Bend sits today. Among the members of this camp was the daughter of the chief, who is remembered as a "squaw of rare beauty". [1] If the description was a true one, then the young princess could have had her pick of any warrior in her own village when she was ready to marry, but the legendary account says Cupid's arrows caused her heart to stray, and so she fell in love with a young chief of another tribe.

In the legendary world, as in the real world, the course of true love quite often never runs smooth, and in this tale it is related that the young maiden's father was not pleased with his daughter's choice of husbands. The hard-hearted chieftain remained opposed to the match, despite the girl's many attempts to soften his opinions. Unable to stand the strain any longer, the inconsolable princess wandered down to the small stream near her village.

The legend doesn't state how long the broken-hearted maiden might have stood on the banks of the little creek. Perhaps, if the tale is a true one, she stood staring into the dark waters for hours, but in the end, according to the account, the distraught princess jumped into the turbulent waters of the stream, near where it enters the river at present-day North Bend, deciding it was better to drown than to be unable to share life with her true love.

Although the Clinton County tale of the star-crossed Indian lovers may sound unique, there are many versions of the same theme that can be found in the northeastern part of the state as well, with one of the most popular accounts preserved in the local legends of the Pocono Mountains of Monroe County. Here, along Route 209 near Marshalls Creek, nature presents one of her most spectacular displays, with cascading waters bursting out of the mountains and roaring over five different waterfalls before reaching the valley one-hundred and seventy-five feet below. It was near this same spot, so says one of the area's legends, that there once lived a beautiful Indian princess named Winona, and it is for her, so says the same legend, that the falls are named.

According to the Monroe County legend of Winona Five Falls, Winona was the daughter of a chief whose tribe was at war with another local tribe. Numbered among the braves in this enemy tribe was the man who was the object of Winona's affection, but affairs of the heart meant little to her father, and despite the princess' pleas the old warrior insisted on vanquishing his foes no matter what the cost. In the end, states the old legend, it would cost him more than he realized.

Unable to bear the thought of what might happen to her beloved if the war were to continue, and realizing she could no longer hope to stop it, the legend relates that Winona slowly made her way up the nearby mountain where the waters seem to explode out of the darkest and coolest recesses of the hills and rush down the rocky ledges to the valley below. Perhaps she had considered this a place where she could sort out her thoughts and discover new proposals to present to her father, but in the end, possibly mesmerized by the undulating mists rising off the foaming stream, the distraught maiden threw herself into the churning waters, which carried her over the sharp rocky cliffs. When the old chief later found the princess' lifeless body at the bottom of the falls it is recalled that he declared an immediate end to the hostilities between his tribe and that of his daughter's lover. [2]

A legend strangely similar to that of the Monroe County tale is often repeated in Carbon County, where tales of Indian warfare were once widely circulated, the most well-known being that of the capture of the Gilbert family by hostile Indians in 1780. Today, however, the most famous Indian episode that can still be heard in this section is the legend of Glen Onoko. Here, in this wild and romantic mountain defile, a tributary of Nesquehoning Creek appears on the top of the Broad Mountains and cascades down through the glen where it spills into the Lehigh River near the small village of Coalport. In its rampant journey, the clear pure mountain stream forms numerous rapids and cascades over countless waterfalls before meeting the calming influence of the river. It is at the highest of these falls, the ninety-foot high Onoko Falls, that the legend of the glen has come to rest, and also, according to that same legend, where the ghost of the legend's young heroine has also found a home.

The Carbon County story is not clear as to when the episode it relates might have occurred, but it must have been sometime in the first half of the eighteenth century when white traders first penetrated the region. About this time it is said that somewhere above where the picturesque town of Mauch Chunk sits today a band of Lenape Indians made their home in one of the many glens and valleys found on the Nesquehoning Mountains. Determined white traders eventually stumbled across the remote Indian encampment, and it was one of these traders that caused the flames of love to burn in the heart of the chief's daughter.

Princess Onoko tried to keep her father ignorant of the growing romance since she knew he would be opposed to any such union, but despite their precautions, the two lovers could not conceal their affections from the wily chieftain forever. When the chief finally realized the depth of the attachment between the two young people, he was appalled. He could not tolerate the thought of his daughter marrying a white trader, and the cruel warrior ordered his braves to take the white man prisoner and then throw him off the highest waterfall on the nearby mountain that frowns down on the site where the Indian village once stood.

Perhaps the old chief's instincts in this case were good ones. Pennsylvania's Provincial Assembly would later note that most of the Indian traders were, "with some few excepted", among "the vilest of our own inhabitants" [3] , but it was not a reason that princess Onoko would have accepted. Devastated by the foul murder of her ideal mate, the distraught maiden decided she could not live without the white trader by her side, and so she made her way up to the same falls where her lover died and jumped to her death.

Today visitors to Onoko Falls can honor the memory of the princess Onoko by burning incense in a stone bowl placed there by an admirer of the legend, but more adventurous people might wish to visit here at night. It is then, so says the old legend, that Onoko's ghost can sometimes be seen floating above the mists of the falls or sitting among the ferns growing on the moss-covered rock shelves on either side of the cascade. [4]

Although princess Onoko's ghost might be a lonely one, readers by now will realize that her story is not unique. The most inquisitive among those who peruse these same lines will also begin to wonder just how true the tales of this type might be. On the other hand, there will be others who dismiss such stories as nothing more than romantic fluff, concocted by gifted story-tellers of an earlier time. But that's the interesting part of investigating legends like this, for no matter what opinion anyone might have about them, everyone seems interested in whether they have a basis in fact or not.

It cannot be denied that there are some historical truths buried in the three Indian princess episodes that have been related in the previous paragraphs, but the motif seems so common that it's hard to believe that all the tales are based on actual events. There's no way to know for sure, of course, but a close look at another such legend from Wyoming County provides some further clues.

When Frank Murphy salvaged a dugout canoe from the bottom of Lake Winola, Wyoming County, one rainy day in 1959, the discovery seemed to revive peoples' interest in that lake's legend. The quaint tale once added a touch of romance and mystery to the little body of water, but over the years the story was almost forgotten as a new order of things replaced the old. With that new age came automobiles, telephones, computers and television sets, and a change in peoples' acceptance of the old tales. Once considered good entertainment and a possible link with the past, legends like that of Lake Winola were relegated to the status of fanciful narratives concocted by colorful raconteurs, but after Murphy discovered his canoe, the story of the lady of the lake took on a new life.

The canoe, or *pirogue,* was obviously of Indian origin, and typical of the dugouts made by Pennsylvania Indians two-hundred and fifty years ago. Archeologists were familiar with the boat type and construction, referring to documented records of previous studies on these types of artifacts. However, the same documentation did not exist for the lake's legend; apparently it was a story that over the years somehow lost its appeal to the newer generations .

According to the narrative that is remembered today, the name that rests on the lake is that of an Indian princess. Not much is remembered about her other than the legendary accounts which state that she was the daughter of a Munsee chieftain named Capouse, or Capoose. Both father and daughter would no doubt have been entirely forgotten over time except for the fact that the old chief's name was given to a mountain range in Luzerne County and his daughter's name was bestowed upon the lake in Wyoming County. Apparently what has been forgotten, however, are the meanings of the two titles.

Even Dr. Donehoo, in his *Indian Villages and Place Names in Pennsylvania,* could not provide an English meaning for the names of Capouse and Winola, stating that in Winola's case at least, "the name is of recent origin, or so badly corrupted that its derivation cannot be discovered".[5] The legend, however, maintains that Winola is a Munsee word meaning "water lily", and that same legend also claims to know how that label came to be bestowed upon the little lake in Wyoming County.

According to history, Capouse was a "civil chief, excelling in the art of agriculture and peace" [6], but the legend of the "pine-fringed" lake claims that he was an inveterate enemy of the white invaders who were settling on Indian lands, and that he led many successful raids on the white settlements that seemed to be appearing more and more often on territory that he considered as rightfully belonging to the Indian. Many white prisoners were supposedly taken when Capouse's warriors swooped down upon the unsuspecting pioneers, and the captives' fate would not have differed much from that of other white people who were captured by Indian war parties.

Typical of any successful Indian raiding party, the Munsee braves would have entered Capouse's village shouting their scalp halloos and victory cries, brandishing their fresh scalps, and herding their prisoners before them. The helpless hostages would next be forced to "run the gauntlet", which consisted of two lines of Indians, with each warrior waiting to strike the runner a hard blow with a stone or club as the prisoner ran between the rows. If a runner survived this ordeal he could then expect one of two fates: to be adopted into the tribe or to be cruelly tortured until life was drained from his body.

Lady Luck and the impression a runner made on the Indians when he, or she, attempted to run the gauntlet were the two determinants that decided a prisoner's fate, and those that weren't killed were held against their will, often becoming adopted sons or daughters of Indian families that had lost their own son or daughter. In some cases an adoptee became so thoroughly assimilated into Indian society that they married a member of the same tribe that had captured them, while in other cases the yearning for freedom was so strong that prisoners attempted to escape even though the chances of success were slim. Thoughts of these types of scenarios must have been swirling through the minds of a small band of captives that, according to the legend of Lake Winola, was brought into Capouse's village one day.

Included among the prisoners was a blond-haired young man who survived the awful ordeal of running the gauntlet. His good looks and his bravery made a particularly favorable impression on Winola, and she became enamored with thoughts of her hero, eventually falling in love with him. Whether or not her feelings were reciprocated is not related, but, irregardless, the young frontiersman had no intention of remaining with the Indians.

One night, when an opportunity finally came, the determined prisoner managed to sneak away. His absence fell hard on Winola, especially as days went by and there was no clue as to his fate. The heart-broken maiden began sitting on the banks of her favorite lake, staring into the water and pining for the blond captive that she had hoped to have as her husband. One bright sunny day, when she could clearly see her own reflection in the placed waters, she suddenly saw the image of the runaway white man's blond hair distinctly appear in the mirror-like surface.

The legend of the lake says that the elated maiden swirled around, thinking she would behold the man of her dreams, who, she hoped, had come back to take her as his wife. However, what she saw was her father standing there, his face gaudily decorated with war paint, and several bloody scalps dangling from his belt. One of the gruesome trophies was the blond locks of the prisoner she had grown to love. Winola's shock and grief were overwhelming, and, says the legend, she turned and threw herself into her father's watery reflection, making no attempt to save herself. Within seconds she sank into the dark waters of the lake she had so often visited, and then she was seen no more. Eventually, says the legend, the lake became known as Lake Winola, in memory of the beautiful Indian princess who drowned herself in its waters. [7]

Those who have done some research into the Winola tale note that maps made in the mid and late 1800's label the lake "Beiches Pond" or "Crooked Pond", rather than Lake Winola. This disregard for the name Winola suggests that the label is, as Doctor Donehoo noted, "of recent origin", and folklorists would agree. Studies done by these scholars have indicated that, at least in the cases of many of the Indian princess suicide legends associated with commercial enterprises, the tales were invented by entrepreneurs hoping to attract tourists. According to Frank Murphy, "every lake seems to have an Indian legend", and he also recalls that someone once did build a large hotel at the body of water now called Lake Winola. [8] It was probably those same people who invented the tale, hoping to lure visitors with the romantic legend.

This blatant invention of stories that some folklorists have labeled "fakelore" does not account for the origins of every Indian princess suicide legend that has surfaced in the Keystone State. In some cases there may be a real event behind the story, but in the case of Lake Winola, at least, that seems doubtful. One final piece of evidence may be of interest to anyone who still believes the Winola legend could be true. If the name Winola means "water lily", as the tale indicates, it would seem that there should at least be some water lilies growing in the lake. There were none at all when I visited there in June of 1975.

Footnote:

The absence of water lilies in Lake Winola could have been used by the "fake-lorist" who invented the tale to create a rather nice ending to his story. He could have said that after Winola drowned in the lake, the once-abundant water lilies died off as well, and ever since then no lilies have grown in the lake, not one.

I shouldn't have even suggested this denouement since I've taken enough liberties with the story as it is. However, I felt that since the legend of Lake Winola has already appeared in print, and since it has dubious origins, I could write the tale out somewhat in my own words without offending too much those who like to see the stories in their purist form.

On the other hand, such an ending would have tied in nicely with another piece of the legend of Glen Onoko. In the woods all around the ravine, and in the glen, rhododendrons grow in profusion. In the spring most of the bushes produce beautiful white flowers, except those on one side of the glen at its base. Here the bushes produce blossoms of pink, and they do so, states the legend, because they were stained with the blood of princess Onoko. [9]

The dugout canoe found in Lake Winola, Wyoming County

BEAR TRACKS

When a two-hundred pound Centre County black bear wandered into downtown State College in search of food one December night in 1999 it caused quite a stir. First the errant bruin walked through a busy parking garage, and then, deciding to get a less-harried base of operations, climbed a tree in front of a florist shop on Allen Street. After dealing with the crowds that gathered to watch the animal, and with the accompanying traffic congestion that followed, local police and state Game Commission officials were finally able to tranquilize the beast and transport it to a remote area. Here the sleepy bear was released so it could roam freely once more.

The officers from the Game Commission were later interviewed for a newspaper article about the event, and were quoted as saying that anyone coming across a bear should not attempt to feed it; but should scare it away instead. This, they said, could "usually" be done by "clapping your hands and hollering."[1] Not everyone confronted by a bear would feel comfortable resorting to noise as a method of chasing it off if the procedure doesn't always work, but the blame should not be placed upon the tactics. Rather the fault lies with the bears themselves, since, by nature, they are a rather unpredictable lot.

When a bear encounters a man out in the wild its reaction can range from frighteningly surly to positively comical, but maybe it's been the lack of respect that the human race has shown the ursine family over the centuries that has caused old bruin to be as fickle as he acts sometimes when he meets one of us. Not an explanation that's likely to be true, since it's an animal's inherent traits that dictate its behavior, but one that does seem to be supported when hunters talk about their face-to-face encounters with these large carnivores.

Meshach Browning, that great Nimrod of the southern Alleghenies of Southwestern Pennsylvania, Maryland and West Virginia from 1795 to 1839, claimed that during one hunting season he "saw twenty bears". Of these, he, by his own account, "killed seventeen, and wounded one", with the last one getting away since it was "shot a little before dark.". [2]

Other hunters were just as merciless. Up in the mountains around present-day Scranton, Elias Scott was making his mark as the Nimrod of the Lackawanna Valley about the same time that Meshach Browning roamed the mountains to the south. Accustomed to taking long hunting trips in the fall, Scott would be gone for up to a week at a time when he went on one of his solitary hunts. When evening came the hardy mountain man would build a campfire to keep wolves and other wild animals at bay, and then he would settle down for the night, his hunting knife and musket by his side, and his leather knapsack rolled up for a pillow.

On one of his expeditions Scott spent the night encamped along the banks of Stafford Meadow Brook in the Moosic Mountains south of Scranton. At daybreak the avid hunter arose and started off into the woods, but he wasn't the only early riser that morning. He hadn't gone too far before he spotted a bear contentedly eating some berries for breakfast. Thinking it would be an easy kill, the marksman aimed and fired.

The bullet found its mark, but it was not a fatal shot, and the enraged bear closed on his assailant. Unable to load his musket before the bear attacked, Scott used the rifle to fend off the enraged animal, backing away from it the whole time. This proved to be an effective defense until the hunter's boot caught on a root, causing him to trip and to fall down. The bear was upon him in an instant, grabbing his left hand in its mouth. Then there took place, in that lonely spot in the mountains, a death struggle between man and beast.

With a presence of mind that came from his many years of taking care of himself in the forest, Scott was able to grab his trusty knife with his free hand and use it to stab the huge bear that was on top of him. This he continued to do until the animal had lost so much blood that "he fell dead upon the mangled hunter". [3]

Aaron Hall was another determined bear hunter who proved to be more than a match for any bear that crossed his path. Born in 1828 in a log cabin that sat along Dick's Run in Centre County, Hall eventually settled along a remote section of the Rattlesnake Pike on the Allegheny Mountains above Unionville. His hunting tactics were much like that of Elias Scott's, and Hall's descendants relate that the old hunter died of pneumonia contracted from nights of sleeping out in cold weather on one of his protracted expeditions.

That same Hall family oral tradition recounts the story of one such outing which involved a bear that left its tracks for the avid hunter to follow. Once he was on a track, Hall was apparently not one to give up until he had killed the animal he was pursuing, and in this case it's recalled that he trailed the bear all the way to the Bear Meadows, today a state natural area preserved near the town of Tusseyville. It was a trek of at least twelve miles, and probably a good bit further since the twelve miles would be the distance measured, as they say in the mountains, "as the crow flies".

Hall shot the bear somewhere in the Bear Meadows and then had to decide what to do with it.. Family accounts say the energetic mountaineer "went and got it in the wagon", but it's not clear whose wagon. If it was his own, then Hall would have had to hike all the way back to Unionville, hitch up his horse and wagon, and then return to the Bear Meadows to get his bear. It would not have been an impossible feat for a man who was used to long hikes in the rugged hills around his brick mansion, which still stands today along the Rattlesnake Pike. [4]

Old-time hunter Laroy Lyman, born in 1821, was yet another Nimrod who never gave the bears a rest. By his own account, Lyman estimated he "killed about 3000 deer and over 400 bear" during his many years of hunting. [5] Lyman, a nationally known hunter whose homestead was located in Roulet, Potter County, kept a diary of his many hunting exploits, and in that interesting journal he mentions his encounters with the bears of the Black Forest of northern Pennsylvania. However, none of these records stand out as a particularly notable bear story worth mentioning in this chapter. The diary's entries are succinct and matter-of-fact, each one just another day in the ordinary life of this rugged mountaineer and old-time hunter. But there were apparently some episodes that Lyman chose, for one reason or another, not to include in his personal accounts. For those stories it is necessary to turn to the oral history handed down through the descendants of the great hunter. When those sources are consulted there is one unusual bear that Lyman was apparently fond of telling about repeatedly. It is a story that was remembered by his children and passed on to his grandchildren, who in turn wrote it down for theirs.

According to that archived account, the "peculiar ways and comic habits" of the black bear were a continuing source of amusement and wonder for the avid Nimrod, but there was one bear in particular, one that seemed far wiser and more comical than the others, that intrigued him the most. And despite his many attempts to shoot and trap this particular bear, Lyman always seemed to be outwitted by the wily bruin. But then one day the frustrated hunter devised a plan for a set-up that he felt sure would net him the quarry that had eluded him for so long.

First he built a three-sided enclosure consisting of "crude rail fences", and then he concealed his bear trap in the middle of the enclosure. He decided not to use bait in the trap, thinking that this would only warn the cagey old beast that something was amiss. Instead Lyman decided to rely on the natural curiosity of the creature to lure him in. However, to increase the appeal of the setup, Laroy also placed one of his old high hats on a stake he had driven into the ground right behind the concealed trap. This interesting fixture, he hoped, would tweak the bear's curiosity even more, leading it right onto the trap.

The next morning the would-be trapper returned to his elaborate snare, hoping to see that the old bear's curiosity had led to its entrapment. As he approached the site of the enclosure he strained to see if the bear had been caught, and then, on the road ahead, he saw a pile of wooden rails. Perched on top was the bear, with the high hat sitting at a cocked angle on its head. Lyman "instantly" knew that the old bruin had detected the trap, dragged the rails out onto the road, and placed the hat on its head as a final outrageous way to mock his adversary. Then, as though adding insult to injury, the bear took off the hat, placed it on the top rail and sat on it, smashing it flat.

The written account concludes by noting that the trapper was so astonished at the sight in front of him that he didn't have time to shoot at the bear when it scrambled down off the wood pile and into the forest. [6] Although it could be argued that this episode might have been a story that Laroy Lyman made up to entertain his grandchildren or to tell to fellow old-timers when they gathered to spin their yarns around the pot-belly stove at Lyman's General Store in Roulet, there are others whose encounters with bears sound just as fantastic.

One such tale is the story of Henry Eyer of Pine Mountain, Clinton County. Born in 1876, "Hen" Eyer eventually took up agriculture as his livelihood, turning his one-hundred and ten acre farm at the head of Spring Run into a garden spot. In his younger days, however, the young Clinton Countian farmed Pine Mountain lands owned by a man named Sam Motter. "California Sam", so named because of money he inherited from his father out in California, was a local character. Motter loved roaming the forests, seemingly preferring the solitude they offered rather than the company of his fellow man. However, he also enjoyed doing outrageous things just to see peoples' reactions, like the time he decided to bridle a bear he had caught in a trap.

Around 1907 or 1908, Motter placed some bear traps out along Robbins Road, near the cranberry swamp, east of the Pine-Loganton Road on top of Pine Mountain. The traps were the typical "steel jaw" variety, and they proved to be effective, netting at least two bears for the trapper. Motter wanted to take home a live speciman, but the first one bit down on his leg as he was trying to release it. In order to free himself, he hit the bear on the head with a hatchet he was carrying, but he misjudged the strength of his blow, striking the bruin so hard that it died on the spot. He didn't have much better luck with the second one.

The second bear had its foot securely caught in the jaws of another of his traps when Motter discovered it. Rather than using the same approach that he tried on the first bear, Sam Motter went home and asked his young farmhand to come along back. With them the two men had a bridle and some ropes, the plan being that Sam would attract the bear's attention on one side while young Eyer was to sneak up on the other, and according to Motter's instructions, "grab that bear by the ears and get that bridle on before he bites you".

"So dad said Sam attracted the bear," recalled Hen Eyer's son, who heard the tale from his father. "He said this bear was looking towards Sam, and he said I snuck up alongside him there, and I grabbed him by the ears; and he said I got the bridle in his mouth."

The two men managed to tighten the bridle, get a rope on the bear, and prod and pull it out to the nearest public road on the mountain. Here they tied it to a tree, and Motter brought it some food and water. It was only a few days before bear season, and Motter wanted to walk his bridled specimen through the streets of Loganton just to show off. However, within a day or two the bear was dead, frightened to death, thought Hen Eyer, from the trauma of its capture. It was a tale the old mountaineer would often tell his son in later years, and that same son assured me that he didn't think his dad "would tell a lie." [7]

In most cases it is the bear that frightens the man, rather than the opposite, but the bear is usually alive when this happens. However, about fifty years ago over in the mountains above Nippenose Valley, Lycoming County, there was a solitary hunter who was almost frightened to death by the bear he had just shot and gutted. It was not a very big bear, between a hundred and a hundred and fifty pounds, and the hunter, who "was pretty wiry at that stage of his life", decided to carry it off the mountain, rather than drag it and risk ruining the hide.

"So what he did, he tied all four feet together with the dragging rope, and then he got down and he put his head up between the feet and he put it on like a knapsack," recalled the hunter's friend. "So then he emptied his rifle, and he was carrying his rifle and he had this bear and its legs around his neck. And the bear itself is around behind him. He'd gutted it, but he didn't take the lungs or anything out – the lungs or liver; he just took the entrails out."

The determined hunter started back down the mountain with his burden on his back, making good time until he came to a "big blowdown log" that had fallen across the path. "It was quite a chore to step up on with this added weight, but he finally got himself balanced and up on this log," continued our storyteller. "Well, then the easiest way down was, he thought, just jump down. You know, just sort of land on both feet. Well, when he did, the bear swung and come back again' him and forced the air out of the lungs. Its head was layin' right there by his ear, and it went 'Woof' into his ear!

"And he said, 'Did you ever see a grown man throw a rifle and run? I just threw the rifle and took off! No matter how fast I run, I wasn't puttin' any distance between the bear and me. It was right with me the whole time!' " [8]

Our storyteller didn't mention at what point the hunter realized he was running from a dead bear, but it was probably after the man ran out of breath and could go no further. Later the bear killer could laugh about the incident, perhaps thinking that bears could indeed be unpredictable, even when they were dead.

Bears have never lost their ability to frighten and amuse people with their unpredictable antics. One October evening about twenty-two years ago a young squirrel hunter was returning to a hunting camp located up in Voneida Gap north of Big Poe Mountain, Centre County, when he noticed a huge black bear sitting in a laurel thicket up ahead. At first it didn't alarm the man since the bear didn't appear to be interested in him. It was almost cute, "sittin' there like a teddy bear; just lookin' around like a big teddy bear would sit on your bed," recalled the man who saw it. He could also see his cabin only a hundred yards ahead, with the reassuring glow from a lantern on a table inside shining through the windows. Then the bear came down out of the laurel thicket and got between the man and the hunting camp.

It was a sight he still remembers to this day. "When I looked at his legs they looked like eight inch stove pipes," he recalls; "I estimated him to be four-hundred to four-hundred and fifty pounds! It was all black except for one big patch of white on its chest."

The bear was the same one the other hunters at the camp had been seeing off and on that year, and now it sat on the road in front of him just sizing him up. Finally the monster got up and lumbered in his direction. It was then that the hunter fully appreciated the bear's size, noticing that it was so massive that "when he walked he just shook!".

Hoping that the bear would not come closer, the frightened Nimrod stood still, until the bear came within five yards and stopped. While shifting its weight from side-to-side the animal eyed the human, snorting at him several times.

"When he did that, that raised the hair on back of my neck," laughed the hunter who experienced the hair-raising episode, and who also recalled that the bear would not let him pass, no matter if he walked left or right when trying to circle around it. At one point the animal raised up on its hind legs and came within three yards of the man, who then pointed his twenty-two magnum rifle at the beast after trying unsuccessfully to scare it away by hollering at it. However, realizing that a rifle this small was "not much killing power for a bear", the cornered hunter lowered his weapon and kept edging around the bruin. Finally he managed to get ahead of his antagonist and into a hemlock clearing, at which point his plan of escape became clearer as well. "I decided "if he's gonna get me now, he's gonna get me from behind!", claimed the lucky escapee. From there it was a mad dash onto the porch and through the cabin door to safety.

The bear didn't linger around the camp once its prey was inside, and no one ever saw it around there again; nor did any one ever hear of its being shot. By now it's no doubt dead from old age, but its descendants are probably the bears that inhabit the same forest today and which people still see from time to time as they drive through the wilds of Voneida Gap. [9]

Bears can be as curious as cats, as the fortunate Voneida Gap hunter now knows , and their curiosity often draws them to humans who would just as soon see them mind their own business. One Clinton County buck hunter certainly still feels that way after inadvertently drawing a curious bear to him one October day during archery season about ten years ago. He had splashed some buck lure , "Tink's number 69", on his boots, and it was early in the morning.

"It was just getting light enough to see maybe ten feet," began the archer. "I was just starting to put tree steps into a tree when I heard this noise coming. I figured 'here's one coming in already', thinking a buck was coming. Then I could see it was a black bear! "

It wasn't a big bear, somewhere around one-hundred and fifty to one-hundred and seventy pounds, but it was fearless. Hollering, and throwing sticks and stones at it didn't seem to bother the bruin in the least, and it got to within ten yards of the hunter before he beat a hasty retreat, leaving his bow, arrows, and a "fanny pack" with the bottle of Tink's 69 in it lying beside the tree.

After "waiting him out", the hunter realized the bear had followed him because of the buck lure it smelled on his boots, and, sure enough, when he finally was able to retrieve his pack and bow, he found that the animal had chewed through the pack and on the seductive bottle of lure, leaving marks from its big teeth on both. Although dismayed at the time that he had lost a morning's hunt because of the bear, it was an experience the archer will never forget and an episode which he now classifies as "a pretty interesting morning" after all. [10]

Another interesting time was had by a hiker who was walking on a mountain in Centre County during the summer of 2000. Out in the one of the wildest parts of southern Centre County, where Tussey Mountain and Thick Head Mountain come together to form an inviting array of airy glens and dark hollows choked with mountain laurel and hemlocks, there is one spot that seems more romantic and more untamed than all the others. The name of this deep hollow is Treaster Kettle, a title that conjures up images of the Hatfield and McCoy country of West Virginia and Kentucky. Although never the scene of feuds like the Hatfield-McCoy wars, it is to this day a place where peace and seclusion can be had by anyone who chooses to penetrate into this mini-wilderness. Even the bears here seem placid at times; at least the black bear that walked through here one July last summer.

The solitary hiker spotted the bruin directly ahead on the Treaster Kettle Road. It was about two-hundred yards away when he first saw it, and he figured it would run away when it saw him. However, the bear kept walking towards him, until it got to within thirty steps, at which point the hiker hollered and threw a handful of crushed stone at it, both to no avail. To the hiker's surprise, the beast kept on coming and then passed by him, not even turning its head to acknowledge his presence, as though the human was of a lower social class unworthy of a even a passing glance .

It appeared the bear had been injured. Its right hip and the right side of its head were "all scarred up", perhaps from a fight with another bear or from being hit by a car. After passing the man, the animal almost immediately left the road and disappeared into the forest, but the experience was still a frightening one. Looking back, the hiker now recalls that the beast "looked like it weighed two hundred pounds after it passed, but six-hundred when it was coming towards me!" [11]

The Treaster Kettle hiker wasn't drinking when he saw the bear on the road ahead, but if he had been, the bear may have looked even bigger when it was approaching. Hard to say what the bear may have thought the human looked like if it had been drinking, but about fifty years ago a group of men would sometimes bring a pet bear to the bar at Orner's Hotel in Milroy, Mifflin County, and let it drink beer. The Pot Licker Flat men who owned the bear, and the other bar patrons, would "get it boomed up", and then, as the evening's form of entertainment, watch the bear stagger around. Old bruin may have been thinking the whole time that his race indeed gets no respect from the human one, but according to the man who recalled seeing the inebriated men load the drunk bear onto the back of their truck when it was time to go home, they "weren't in much better shape than the bear!" [12]

FOOTNOTES TO THE TALES

I. Will-o'-the-Wisp

1. Bumbaugh, L. W. (born: 1910), recorded 8/22/89
2. Treaster, Vince (born: 1922), recorded 11/5/88
3. Korson, George, *Black Rock, Mining Folklore of the Penna. Dutch*, 161
4. Tantaquidgeon, Gladys, *Folk Medicine of the Delaware*, 101
5. Bayard, Samuel P. (born: 1908), recorded 12/26/77
6. Auman, Mrs. Arthur (born: ?), recorded 10/31/81
7. Henry, Dennis (born: 1956), recorded 7/3/97
8. Varner, Harold (born:3/29/47), interviewed 7/97

II. The Ghostly Lantern

1. Dean, Randy (born: 2/14/1963), recorded 6/4/99
2. Daup, William (born: ?), recorded 9/17/89
3. "Have you seen John Horning's lantern glowing at night?", article appearing in the *Lewistown Sentinel*, Lewistown, Pa., 10/97
4. "Return to the McVeytown Ghost Light, 1989", by Beth Kibler, appeared in *The Stone Arch Players on Cue Monthly* newsletter, Mifflintown, Pa., October, 1989
5. Henry, Dennis (born: 1956), recorded 7/3/97
6. Varner, Harold (born:3/29/47), interviewed 7/97

III. Punxsutawney

1. Benton, W., publisher, *Encyclopedia Britannica Micropedia – Vol. IV, 755*
2. Meginness, John F., *Otzinachson*, 273
3. Meginness, John F., *ibid.*, 417-418
4. Fletcher, Stevenson W. *Pennsylvania Agriculture and Country Life, 1640-1840,* 75
5. Godcharles, Frederic A., *Pennsylvania: Political & Civil History,* 229
6. Pennypacker, Samuel W., *Pennsylvania, The Keystone*, 14
7. Heckewelder, Rev. John, *History of the Indian Nations*, 209
8. Heckewelder, Rev. John, *ibid.*, 233-234
9. Pennsylvania Writers' Project, *Pennsylvania, A Guide to the Keystone State*, 478
10. Meginness, John F., *op. cit.*, 416-418

IV. A Trophy Buck
1. Vonada, Clifford (born: 8/23/1905), recorded 4/13/98
2. McKnight, W. J., *Pioneer Outline History of Northwestern Pa.,* 18
3. Tome, Philip, *Pioneer Life or Thirty Years a Hunter,* 109
4. Blackman, Emily C.
History of Susquehanna County, Pennsylvania, 418
5. Browning, Meshach,, *Forty-four Years of the Life of a Hunter,* 392-395
6. Blackman, Emily C., *op.cit.,* 153
7. Ripka, Jared B. (born: 1885), interviewed 8/27/71 & 2/2/74
8. *McKnight, W. J., op. cit.,* 128
9. Poust, Dave (born: 1930), recorded 6/21/98

V. God's Warriors
1. Linn, John Blair, *History of Centre and Clinton Counties,* 613 (quotes a newspaper account which appeared in the January 2, 1873, edition of the *Clinton County Democrat*)
2. Tibbens, George (born: 6/5/1913), recorded 7/10/99
3. Montgomery, Thomas L., editor,
Frontier Forts of Pennsylvania - Vol. I, 553
4. Sipe, C. Hale, *The Indian Wars of Pennsylvania,* 463-466
5. Sassaman, Grant N., editor, *Pennsylvania, A Guide to the Keystone State, 443 (See also:* Egle, William H., *History of Pennsylvania,* 849)
6. Sipe, C. Hale, *The Indian Chiefs of Pennsylvania,* 126-127
7. Swetnam, George, *Pittsylvania Country,* 124
8. Malone, Blaine (born: 1903), *History of Coburn. (*Privately published manuscript). Interviewed Mr. Malone on 10/23/80 & 4/21/81
9. Bartges, Paul (born: ??), interviewed 8/28/72
Some of the facts behind this story were also taken from " The Rebellion In the North", a series of newspaper articles, written by Mrs. Myrtle Magargel, which appeared in the *Centre Daily Times,* of Bellefonte, Pa., February 23 through February 26, 1937
10. Barnhart, Hannah (born: 1823) - from a manuscript written for her descendants in 1898 (copy given to the author by Mr. Ellis Hall of Unionville, Pennsylvania, in August of 1999)
11. Linn, John Blair, *History of Centre and Clinton Counties,* 127, 158
12. Serff, John J., "General, Governor, Judge - James A. Beaver",
Centre County Heritage, 1956-1975, 11

VI. Man's Best Friend(ly ghost)
1. Bumbaugh, L. W. (born: 1910), interviewed 8/27/72; recorded 8/22/89
2. Brendle, Thomas R., and Troxell, William S., "Pennsylvania German Folk Tales, Legends, Once-upon-a-time Stories, Maxims, and Sayings"' *Proceedings of the Pennsylvania German Society – Vol. L.*, 124
3. Wharton, Anne Hollingsworth, *In Old Pennsylvania Towns,* 102
4. Fiedel, Dorothy B., *Haunted Lancaster County Pennsylvania,* 9
5. Korson, George, *Black Rock,* 302
6. Lepovetsky, Howard (born: ?), recorded 10/20/97
7. Brown, Harry Jr., (born: 1926), recorded 5/5/88 & 5/21/89
8. Hardwick, Charles, *Traditions, Superstitions and Folk-Lore,* pp 173-175
9. Brendle and Troxell, *op. cit.,* 124

VII. Ravens' Knob
1. Fletcher, Stevenson W. *Pennsylvania Agriculture and Country Life, 1640-1840,* 468-70
2. McKnight, W. J., *Pioneer Outline History of Northwestern Pa.,* 380
3. Magargel, Myrtle, "The History of Pleasant Gap ", installment #15 from a series of sixty installments which were published in *The Centre Daily Times* of Bellefonte from March 16 through June 20, 1936
4. Beers, Paul B., *The Pennsylvania Sampler,* 49
5. Linn, John Blair, *History of Centre and Clinton Counties,* 411
6. Information also taken from a tourist pamphlet entitled "Millheim Pennsylvania Invites You To Visit Beautiful Penn's Valley", sponsored by the Millheim Lions Club – publication date unknown.
7. Musser, Clarence (born: 5/12/1884), interviewed 8/28 & 11/12/71
8. Linn, John Blair, *History of Centre and Clinton Counties,* pp. 7,25,403
9. Shedd, Nancy S. (editor), *Rung's Chronicles of Pennsylvania History,* 91
10. Quinn, Arthur H., editor, *Edgar Allan Poe, Complete Tales and Poems,* 80
11. Korson, George, *Black Rock,* 84

VIII. Big Cats of the Big Woods
1. Rhoads, Samuel N., *Mammals of Pennsylvania and New Jersey,* 135
2. McKnight, W. J., *Pioneer Outline History of Northwestern Pa.,* 176-177
3. Blackman, Emily C., *History of Susquehanna County,* 119
4. Aldrich, Lewis Cass, *History of Clearfield County,* 459
5. Linn, John Blair, *History of Centre and Clinton Counties,* 585
6. Tome, Philip, *Pioneer Life or Thirty Years a Hunter,* 111
7. Blackman, *op. cit.,* 305
8. Hollister, H., *History of the Lackawanna Valley,* 291
9. McKnight, W. J., *op. cit.,* 517
10. Letter sent to Harris Breth by Rosie Bailor, dated April 2nd, 1959
11. Rhoads, *op. cit.,* 130

IX. The Beaverdam Witch

1. Elder, Helen (born: 5/9/1921), recorded 6/5/98
2. Ingram, John H.,
   The Haunted Homes and Family Traditions of Great Britain, 158
3. Breon, Evelyn (born: 1918), recorded 5/5/88
4. Rowles, Ray (born: 1/27/33), recorded 5/26/88
5. Meyer, Nedra, recorded 6/6/99
6. Fletcher, Stevenson W.
   Pennsylvania Agriculture and Country Life, 1640-1840, 504
7. Tantaquidgeon, Gladys, *Folk Medicine of the Delaware,* 90
8. Bilger, Dave (born: 8/7/1907), recorded 12/5/99
9. Bayard, Samuel P. (born: 1908), recorded 12/26/77

X. Council Rocks

1. Allingham, William, from his poem entitled "Fairyland"
2. Musser, Clarence (born: 5/12/1884), interviewed 8/28 & 11/12/71
3. Blunt, A. M (editor)., *Gregg Township Bi-centennial,* 33
4. Bright, Mary (born: 4/7/1913), recorded 1/26/90
5. Frazier, Nancy (born: 5/9/1952), interviewed 8/72, recorded 9/17/90
6. Linn, John Blair, *History of Centre and Clinton Counties,* 290
7. Zettle, Roy (born: 9/19/1896), recorded 6/23/90
8. Smith, Doris (born: 7/12/1931), recorded 8/25/96
9. Heckewelder, Rev. John, *History of the Indian Nations,* 100
10. Trento, Salvatore M., *The Search For Lost America,* 35

XI. Frozen in Time

1. Henretta, J. E., *Kane and the Upper Allegheny,* 27
2. Grimm, Herbert L. and Roy, Paul L. *Human Interest Stories of the Three Days' Battles at Gettysburg, 41*
3. Details taken from an article entitled "80 years ago, warring troops paused for Christmas". Written by Graham Heathcote, the piece appeared in the *Intelligencer Journal* of Lancaster, Pa., on 12/24/91 and was based on the book *Christmas Truce* by Malcolm Brown and Shirley Seaton; published in 1984.
4. Sheads, Col. Jacob M. (born: 4/17/1910), recorded 7/28/89
5. Coco, Gregory A., *On the Bloodstained Field II,* 112
6. Sheads, Col. Jacob M., editor,
   A Pictorial History of the Battle of Gettysburg, 19
7. Sheads, Col. Jacob M. (born: 4/17/1910), recorded 7/28/89
8. Hain, H. H., *History of Perry County, Pennsylvania,* 552

XII. *Spitzbuben*

1. Mitchell, Edwin V, *It's an old Pennsylvania Custom,* 120
2. Linn, John Blair, *History of Centre and Clinton Counties,* 352
3. Linn, *ibid.,* 62
4. Shedd, Nancy S. (editor), *Rung's Chronicles of Pennsylvania History, Volume II,* 270-71
5. Kinter, Ralph (born: 1/5/1915), recorded 6/6/89
6. Lee, J. Marvin, "Shoot and Be Damned", article appeared in *Town & Gown* magazine of State College, dated April, 1980
7. Stephens, James (born: 1924), recorded 12/23/89
8. Zettle, Roy (born: 9/19/1896), recorded 6/23/90
9. Felleman, Hazel, editor, *Poems That Live Forever, 16*

XIII. *Maids of the Mist*

1. Meginness, John F., *Otzinachson,* 86
   (also see Linn's *History of Centre & Clinton Counties,* p. 584)
2. The Pike County version of this legend was obtained from "The Legend of Winona", included in a tourist pamphlet, entitled *In the Poconos ... Winona 5 Falls,* obtained by the author when he visited there in 1975.
   The Carbon County version of the legend can be found on page 489 of *Pennsylvania, A Guide to the Keystone State,* Grant N. Sassaman, editor.
3. Hanna, Charles A., *The Wilderness Trail, Volume 2,* 307
4. Details on the Glen Onoko legend were obtained from a story entitled "The Falls of Glen Onoko", by Chris Royer. The article appeared in a tourist newspaper published in December 1998 at Jim Thorpe, Pa. Other details about the legend were heard on WPSX radio's folk song show September, 1999.
5. Donehoo, Dr. George P., *Indian Villages and Place Names in Pennsylvania,* p. 259
6. Hollister, H., *History of the Lackawanna Valley,* 29
7. Sassaman, Grant N., editor, *Pennsylvania, A Guide to the Keystone State,* 362
8. Murphy, Frank (born: 2/1925), recorded 1/27/90
9. This additional information on the legend of Glen Onoko was found on the web page for Jim Thorpe, Pa. (www.jtasd.k12.pa.us/jimthorpe/falls/History)

XIV. *Bear Tracks*

1. Wengerd, Erin R., "Black bear checks out downtown, climbs a tree"; article which appeared in the *Centre Daily Times* of State College on 12/6/99
2. Browning, Meshach,, *Forty-four Years of the Life of a Hunter,* 152
3. Hollister, H., *History of the Lackawanna Valley,* 282
4. Hall, Ellis (born: 1919), recorded 8/7/99
5. Lyman, Robert R. Sr., *History of Roulet, Pa., 83*
   Details on Laroy Lyman's life and times were also obtained from a copy of

his diary and memoirs. Laroy's personal estimate of his hunting record appears on page four of the copy provided to me by Ms. Krista Lyman of Roulet, the old hunter's great great granddaughter.

6. The account of Laroy Lyman's experience with the wily bear appears on page 6 of the document mentioned in 5.
7. Eyer, Alvin (born: 1/5/1915), recorded 8/14/99
8. Poust, Dave (born: 1930), recorded 2/27/98
9. Arney, Lance (born: 6/28/50), recorded 7/4/00
10. Sodergren, Richard (born: 1/15/42), recorded 5/12/00
11. Ralston, Gil (born: 11/26/23), interviewed (telephone) 9/12/00
12. Weidensaul, Craig (born:), interviewed (telephone) 8/8/00

BIBLIOGRAPHY

Aldrich, Lewis Cass, *History of Clearfield County, Pennsylvania,* Syracuse, N. Y. , D. Mason and Company, 1887

Beers, Paul B., *The Pennsylvania Sampler,* Harrisburg, Pa., Stackpole Books, 1970

Benton, William, publisher, *Encyclopedia Britannica, 15th Edition* Chicago, Ill., Encyclopedia Britannica, Inc., 1975

Blackman, Emily C., *History of Susquehanna County, Pennsylvania* Philadelphia, Pa., Claxton, Remsen & Haffelfinger, 1873

Blunt, A. M., editor, *Gregg Township Bicentennial, Two Hundred Years Remembered,* Gregg Township Civic Action Committee, Spring Mills, Pa., 1977

Brendle, Thomas R., and Troxell, William S., `Pennsylvania German Folk Tales, Legends, Once-a-upon-a-time Stories, Maxims, and Sayings`, *Proceedings of the Pennsylvania German Society, Vol. L,* Norristown, Pa., Pennsylvania German Society, 1944

Browning, Meshach, *Forty-four Years of the Life of a Hunter,* Reprint of the 1859 edition, Baltimore, Gateway Press, Inc., 1993

Centre County Historical Society, *Centre County Heritage, 1956-75,* (compilation of twenty years of the society's quarterly publication of the same name), Bellefonte, Pa., 1975

Coco, Gregory, *On the Bloodstained Field II* Gettysburg, Pa., Thomas Publications, 1989

Donehoo, Dr. George P., *History of Indian Village and Place Names in Pennsylvania,* Harrisburg, Pa., The Telegraph Press, 1928

Fiedel, Dorothy Burtz, *Haunted Lancaster County Pennsylvania, Ghosts and Other Strange Occurrences,* Ephrata, Pa., Science Press, 1994

Felleman, Hazel, editor, *Poems That Live Forever,* Garden City, N. Y., Doubleday and Company, 1965

Fletcher, Stevenson W., *Pennsylvania Agriculture & Country Life, 1640-1840,* Harrisburg, Pennsylvania Historical and Museum Commission, 1971

Godcharles, Frederic A., *Pennsylvania: Political, Governmental, Military, and Civil* New York, N. Y., The American Historical Society, 1933

Grimm, Herbert L., and Roy, Paul L., *Human Interest Stories of the Three Days' Battles at Gettysburg* Gettysburg, Pa., Times and News Publishing Co., 1927

Hain, H. H., *History of Perry County, Pennsylvania* Harrisburg, Pa., Hain-Moore Co., 1922

Hanna, Charles A., *The Wilderness Trail,* New York, N. Y., AMS Press, 1911

Hardwick, Charles, *Traditions, Superstitions, and Folk-lore, (Chiefly Lancashire and the North of England),* Manchester, England, A. Ireland & Co., 1872

Heckewelder, Rev. John, *History, Manner, & Customs of the Indian Nations,* Philadelphia, Lippincott's Press, 1876

Henretta, J. E., *Kane and the Upper Allegheny,* Philadelphia, Winston & Co., 1929

Hollister, H., *History of the Lackawanna Valley,* Scranton, Pa., M. Norton, bookseller and stationer, third edition, 1875

Ingram, John H., *The Haunted Homes and Family Traditions of Great Britain,* London, Reeves and Turner, 1905

Korson, George, *Black Rock, Mining Folklore of the Pennsylvania Dutch* Baltimore, Md., Johns Hopkins Press, 1960

Linn, John Blair, *History of Centre and Clinton Counties, Pennsylvania,* Philadelphia, Louis H Everts Co., 1883

Lyman,, Robert R. Sr., *History of Roulet, Pennsylvania and the Life of Burrel Lyman (The Founder),* Coudersport, Pa., Potter County Historical Society., 1967

McKnight, William J., *Pioneer Outline History of Northwestern Pennsylvania,* Philadelphia, Lippincott Co., 1905

Meginess, John F., *Otzinachson, A History of the West Branch Valley,* Williamsport, Pa., Gazette Printing House, 1889

Mitchell, Edwin V., *It's an old Pennsylvania Custom* New York, N. Y., Vanguard Press, Inc., 1947

Montgomery, Thomas L., *Frontier Forts of Pennsylvania,* Harrisburg, Pa., Pennsylvania Historical Commission, 1915

Muffley, Adjt. J. W., editor, *The Story of Our Regiment, A History of the 148th Pennsylvania Volunteers,* Des Moines, Iowa, Kenyon Printing and Manufacturing Company, 1904

Pennypacker, Samuel W., *Pennsylvania, The Keystone, A Short History* Philadelphia, Pa., Christopher Sower Co., 1915

Quinn, Arthur H., editor, *Edgar Allen Poe, Complete Tales and Poems,* New York, N. Y., Barnes & Noble, 1992

Rhoads, Samuel N., *Mammals of Pennsylvania and New Jersey,* Lancaster, Pa., Wickersham Printing Co., 1903

Sassaman, Grant N., *Pennsylvania, A Guide to the Keystone State,* Pennsylvania Writers' Project New York, Oxford University Press, 1940

Sheads, Col. Jacob M., editor, *A Pictorial History of the Battle of Gettysburg* Gettysburg, Pa., TEM, Inc., 1978

Shedd, Nancy S., editor,
Rung's Chronicles of Pennsylvania History,
Huntingdon, Pa., Huntingdon County Historical Society, 1984

Sipe, C. Hale, *The Indian Chiefs of Pennsylvania,*
Butler, Pa., Ziegler Printing Co., 1927

Sipe, C. Hale, *The Indian Wars of Pennsylvania,*
Harrisburg, Pa., The Telegraph Press, 1931

Swetnam, George, *Pittsylvania Country,*
New York, N. Y., Duell, Sloan & Pearce, Inc., 1951

Tantaquidgeon, Gladys, *Folk Medicine of the Delaware,*
Harrisburg, Pa., Pennsylvania Historical Commission, 1972

Tome, Phillip, *Pioneer Life, or Thirty Years a Hunter,*
Baltimore, Md., Gateway Press, 1989, reprint of the 1854 edition.

Trento, Salvatore M.,
The Search For Lost America, (The Mysteries of the Stone Ruins),
Chicago, Ill., Contemporary Books, Inc., 1978

Wharton, Anne Hollingsworth, *In Old Pennsylvania Towns,*
Philadelphia, Pa., J. B. Lippincott, 1920

THE END